Longman School
Drama

The Search for Odysseus
by Charles Way

PEARSON
Longman

Pearson Education Limited
Edinburgh Gate
Harlow
Essex
CM20 2JE
England
and Associated Companies throughout the World

The Search for Odysseus was originally published in 1998 by Aurora Metro Press in the anthology *Young Blood: plays for young performers*, ed. Sally Goldsworthy

This educational edition first published by Pearson Education 2007

Activities by Emma Lee

Cover image © Kevin Fleming/CORBIS

ISBN 978-1-4058-5683-6

Second Impression 2008

Printed in Malaysia (CTP-VVP)

The Publisher's policy is to use paper manufactured from sustainable forests.

Contents

Characters

TELEMACHUS

ATHENE

PENELOPE

EURYMACHUS

ODYSSEUS

EURYCLEIA

ALCINOUS

LAODOMUS

CYCLOPS

ACHILLES

CALYPSO

ARETE

NAUSICAA

MESSENGER

CAST / CHORUS / CALYPSO'S HELPERS

The play can be performed by six actors doubling.

ACT ONE

Music. ATHENE, *Daughter of Zeus, enters dressed as a beggar.*

ATHENE   Once upon a time in the land of Greece,
On an island called Ithaca
there lived a man named...

CAST   Odysseus.

Enter ODYSSEUS.

ATHENE   Odysseus was the King of Ithaca,
a brave man, a good man
and when his country called him to war
he put on his bronze armour
picked up his sharpened spear
and led his men down
to the long black ships
which lay in wait on the cold tide
and his wife wept to see him go.

A light rises on PENELOPE *who holds a baby in her arms.*

PENELOPE   My husband.

ODYSSEUS   Penelope.

PENELOPE   Please do not go.

ODYSSEUS   I have no choice.

PENELOPE   Your son, your son.

ODYSSEUS   I'll be home before he's a year old, I promise.

PENELOPE   You promise?

Silence.

1

ODYSSEUS   If I don't come back by the time my son has grown his first beard then consider me as dead and marry again, if you wish, a younger man.

The cast representing soldiers and people of Ithaca, laugh at this last remark.

PENELOPE   You are my husband. How can you joke at a moment like this?

ODYSSEUS   Because it won't happen. I'll come home to you and to my beloved Ithaca. I shall see the smoke rising from the chimney and my son will run down to the harbour to greet me.

PENELOPE   Not if he's only a year old my husband.

ODYSSEUS   (*he smiles*) Within a year the bell will ring out with news of our victory.

A WOMAN   Look – Odysseus.

Music. Then as if in the sky above the harbour, a small sparrow is chased and crushed in the talons of an eagle. This may be represented through percussive sound.

A SOLDIER   What does it mean Odysseus?

ODYSSEUS   It's a good omen my friends. The sparrow represents our enemy, the Trojans. We the Greeks are the eagle. We will crush the enemy in our mighty talons, win the war and be home for supper.

ALL   Odysseus!

ODYSSEUS kisses PENELOPE with love and passion and then he holds up his baby son.

ODYSSEUS   My son, listen for the bell, then I will come home with my arms full of gold, treasures, beyond your wildest dreams – and all for you.

ATHENE	And with these words, brave Odysseus, good Odysseus, set sail for a distant land far across the wine dark sea.
CAST	Odysseus – Odysseus.

Exit ODYSSEUS.

PENELOPE *stands looking out to sea.*

ATHENE	And his son saw him go but did not understand the meaning of the horizon.
PENELOPE	Hush, hush little one, your father will be home soon, home soon, home soon.

The music continues low and foreboding containing a sense of the war far away.

ATHENE	But the war did not last a year or even two, or three, or four, or five, or six or seven or eight or nine and all the long years Penelope waited. And her son grew tall, and his name was, Telemachus.
CAST	Telemachus.

Enter TELEMACHUS *as a ten-year-old boy. He comes on brandishing a sword fighting an invisible enemy.* EURYMACHUS, *his mother's suitor, watches him from the shadows.*

TELEMACHUS	Odysseus the hero and his friend the angry Achilles are in a tight spot. Back to back they face one hundred Trojans. The Trojans charge. The swords of the heroes never cease – blood and limbs fill the air – the Trojans die horrible deaths. (*This he acts out.*) At last there are only two men left standing, Odysseus and Achilles – but then an arrow flies. (*He falls.*)

'My heel my heel' the hero cries, and as he dies he calls out. 'Farewell Odysseus, farewell – my friend'. (*As Achilles, he dies.*)

EURYMACHUS *applauds.*

TELEMACHUS What do you want?

EURYMACHUS The other lads are playing in the courtyard, why don't you join them? (*He picks up* TELEMACHUS' *sword which is wooden.*)

TELEMACHUS Give my sword back.

EURYMACHUS A fine sword.

TELEMACHUS Give it back.

EURYMACHUS I came to talk to you – about your mother.

TELEMACHUS One day, my father will come home and cut your head off.

EURYMACHUS Here, let's play together, you and I. (*He offers* TELEMACHUS *his sword back.*)

TELEMACHUS I don't want to play with you.

EURYMACHUS Don't be rude, Telemachus.

TELEMACHUS It's my house, I'll be rude if I want.

EURYMACHUS Come let's spar together like Father and Son. (*He throws down the sword which* TELEMACHUS *picks up.*)

Come attack me. (*He walks towards* TELEMACHUS *who is very scared.*) We're only playing aren't we? (TELEMACHUS *drops his sword.* EURYMACHUS *then puts his own sword against his throat.*) Understand this Telemachus. I wouldn't let a man live who spoke to me as you have spoken to me. But you are not a man –

TELEMACHUS My father...

EURYMACHUS Your father is dead.

TELEMACHUS No – no.

EURYMACHUS	And I will marry your mother.
TELEMACHUS	No! (EURYMACHUS *removes the sword.*) My father is alive. He will come home and sweep you from the house like so many dead leaves.
EURYMACHUS	Perhaps it would be better for your mother if he were dead. Have you thought of that? Or are you too young to understand? Love can grow cold you know.

A bell rings.

TELEMACHUS	The bell. There must be some mistake. (*pause*) It still rings.

PENELOPE *enters.*

PENELOPE	Telemachus. The war. The war is over. (*She embraces her son.*)
TELEMACHUS	(*turns to* EURYMACHUS) Now, now we shall see. My father will have your head.

Enter EURYCLEIA.

EURYCLEIA	My lady. A messenger is at the gate.
PENELOPE	Let him in, let him in – no wait. Give him food and drink. We must not forget ourselves.
EURYCLEIA	Yes my lady.
PENELOPE	It doesn't seem possible and yet the bell still rings. Is it really true do you think?
TELEMACHUS	It must be. It has to be. (*They embrace again.*)

Enter EURYCLEIA.

EURYCLEIA	The poor man will not eat. He will not drink but begs to see you now.
PENELOPE	Then let him in, no wait – let him bathe and give him clean clothes…

TELEMACHUS   Mother.

PENELOPE   Yes – let him in – let him in.

EURYCLEIA *exits momentarily and she and the* MESSENGER *enter.*

MESSENGER   My lady, I see by your smile the news has younger legs than me.

PENELOPE   It's true then.

MESSENGER   As true as I stand here. The war with Troy is over!

Silence.

PENELOPE   Good. And – did we win?

MESSENGER   (*laughs*) Aye. Troy is no more than dust. Its men are dead, the women and children sold into slavery.

PENELOPE *nods, unsure how to react.*

TELEMACHUS   My father?

MESSENGER   Your father is safe and well. I saw him set sail for home in his own ship with twenty trusted men.

TELEMACHUS   (*punching the air*) Yes! Yes!

MESSENGER   Brave Odysseus. We all rejoice to speak his name. Not a single Greek would be home yet but for him. Your husband's wits have saved us all.

TELEMACHUS   How? Tell me everything in every detail. Mother?

PENELOPE   Yes – go on.

MESSENGER   Odysseus of the nimble wits is what we call him now for he devised a plan so clever, so full of cunning. Under his orders we made it seem as if the war had broken all our hearts. For ten years we had camped outside the city walls of Troy and won nothing but wounds and grey hairs. Great warriors like Achilles had been killed, so our giving up was not hard for the

Trojans to believe. One morning as they awoke they found the field of battle empty, our camp fires out, our ships gone. They cried out in joy, 'The Greeks have fled, we have defeated them!', not knowing that all our soldiers armed and ready to kill were hiding on an island just a few miles away. The Trojans came out of the city and danced in and out of our empty tents. 'Here camped the merciless Achilles, there the clever Odysseus'. Now gone it seemed, all gone except an offering that we had made to the Gods and left behind.

TELEMACHUS   What kind of offering?

MESSENGER   A horse. A huge wooden horse. It was made from sawn firwood, and its belly was a cavernous womb large enough to hold twenty soldiers armed to the teeth. Your father was among them.

TELEMACHUS   Inside the belly of the wooden horse.

MESSENGER   The Trojans in their joy pushed the horse through the gates of their mighty city and for the first time in ten years, after all the wasted blood of the battlefield, by one trick we too were inside. All night the Trojans drank and danced and when at last they fell asleep your father, your husband, glad to be free, led out his men with stealth. He slew the sentry with one silent blow.

TELEMACHUS   Yes!

MESSENGER   Opened the gates of Troy from the inside and the whole of our army, bristling with knives and swords poured in under cover of darkness.

TELEMACHUS   And then…?

MESSENGER   (*pause*) And then the moon hid her eyes. No tongue can describe the terrible slaughter of that night.

TELEMACHUS	How many did my father kill?
PENELOPE	Telemachus!
TELEMACHUS	My father is a soldier, and a hero amongst men. They should call him a God.
MESSENGER	Aye many of the common soldiers do for he has brought us home and we are glad.
PENELOPE	Messenger. Thank you. Where is the fleet that brings my husband home?
MESSENGER	There was a storm just a few miles from the coast of Troy which scattered the fleet, so each ship will make its way alone. Your husband's ship was among the fastest. The first mast on the horizon should belong to him and you.
PENELOPE	Eurycleia, bring the Messenger some food now. He will stay with us tonight.
MESSENGER	My lady, I will resist. I have a son who was just a few days old when the war began. I haven't seen him for ten years, and I've another day's walk to my farm, before I do.
PENELOPE	May the Gods bless you.
MESSENGER	And your house.

Exit MESSENGER.

PENELOPE	Ten years? Why not ten months, ten days, ten minutes?…

EURYMACHUS *goes to comfort her.*

TELEMACHUS	Leave her alone.
PENELOPE	Telemachus, go and prepare to meet your father. Go on.

Exit TELEMACHUS.

EURYMACHUS	I'm glad the war's over Penelope.
PENELOPE	Yes. Perhaps you should leave before my husband comes home.
EURYMACHUS	Are you ashamed?
PENELOPE	No.
EURYMACHUS	Then I'll stay and greet him.

Music. A fanfare.

TELEMACHUS enters wearing a fine robe.

EURYCLEIA enters and gives PENELOPE a fine robe also.

TELEMACHUS	Mother! There are ships on the horizon. Can you see them?
PENELOPE	(*gently*) Yes, I see them.
ATHENE	One by one the ships sailed home from war returning swiftly on the welcoming tide. Husbands and wives, fathers and sons were reunited. Each day another boat came home.
TELEMACHUS	Sailor, have you seen my father's ship?
SAILOR	No master, but he should be close behind.
TELEMACHUS	He will come home now won't he mother? Now the war's over.
ATHENE	Each day mother and son gazed out to sea until all those who had escaped sheer destruction, either by land or sea came home, all but one man alone.
CAST	Odysseus.
TELEMACHUS	Father! Father! Where is he? What could keep him?
PENELOPE	The sea.

TELEMACHUS   No! (*He calls out again.*) Father!

Silence.

Exit TELEMACHUS.

PENELOPE *goes to a large spinning wheel. She begins to spin and to sing.*

PENELOPE   Many years I have waited
On this cold, lonely shore
Many tears I have wasted
for a man and his war.
Now my eye has forgotten
the shape of his face
The sea has devoured him
and left me no trace.

She continues to spin indicating that she has become withdrawn and introspective. EURYMACHUS *watches her.*

ATHENE   Again the years passed by, and at fourteen years old, Telemachus showed the first signs of his first beard.

TELEMACHUS *enters, once again he fights invisible enemies.*

EURYMACHUS *enters.*

EURYMACHUS   Come on Telemachus – we're only playing aren't we? (TELEMACHUS *drops his sword and* EURYMACHUS *smiles.*) It's past your bedtime – Telemachus. Go on. (TELEMACHUS *picks up his sword and goes to his bed. He plays with a wooden horse from which soldiers descend.*)

EURYMACHUS   (*goes to* PENELOPE) Penelope? (*silence*) Penelope.

PENELOPE   Yes?

EURYMACHUS   Have you spoken to your son yet?

PENELOPE   What about?

EURYMACHUS	About the matter we discussed.
PENELOPE	I've been busy.
EURYMACHUS	So I see. (*pause*) What are you making?
PENELOPE	I'm not sure. It will turn into something eventually.
EURYMACHUS	Why don't you speak to him tonight? (*silence*) Penelope?
PENELOPE	Mmm?
EURYMACHUS	We must move forward, with our lives together. If we wait any longer I fear…
PENELOPE	(*sharply*) For what? For whom?
EURYMACHUS	For you. Every day you sit and spin not knowing what you make. Each day your mind travels to some dreamland where I cannot follow. (*pause*) Penelope, do not waste your life. The time has come for you and your son to accept that Odysseus is dead. Drowned at sea.
PENELOPE	I have not heard that.
EURYMACHUS	How would one hear it? Unless the sea spoke. He is drowned and all his men too.
PENELOPE	But still, we don't know that for sure, do we?
EURYMACHUS	Penelope, I am a man, alive. I am here. I have been here through all your loneliness.
PENELOPE	Yes, you've been here, Eurymachus, eating his oxen, drinking his wine, sitting in his chair. (*pause*) I'm sorry… I…
EURYMACHUS	If by any chance your husband still lives, he has deserted you and your son. (*He grabs her arm.*) All that I have waited for is mine. (*He lets her go realising he has said too much.* PENELOPE *starts to unravel her*

11

work.) What are you doing? Stop. Stop. (*pause*) Are you sick?

PENELOPE   So many died in that long war, Eurymachus. So many.

EURYMACHUS   But your work is all undone.

PENELOPE   (*She smiles.*) I can make it again, it's easy.

He backs away. Then sees EURYCLEIA *has been watching. He exits.* EURYCLEIA *takes a small chain from around her neck. On it is a small bottle which she now gives to* PENELOPE. TELEMACHUS *throughout this scene has been playing in his bedroom.* TELEMACHUS *stands on the bed, sword in hand.*

TELEMACHUS   Odysseus the hero and his friend the angry Achilles are in a tight spot. Back to back they face one hundred Trojans… (*He then sits dejected.*) Odysseus and Achilles. (*He lies back on the bed.*)

Suddenly there is a crack of thunder. A change of lighting produces a dark stage. A savage wind blows. TELEMACHUS *screams and retreats to the top of his bed holding a pillow in front of him. Two masked soldiers enter – in dance – and then face each other.*

TELEMACHUS   (*in hope*) Odysseus and Achilles…

Another crack of thunder, then the two masked soldiers begin to fight.

No! No!

Spears and shields clash violently against each other then suddenly ODYSSEUS *falls.* ACHILLES *stands over him spear raised for the kill – silence.* TELEMACHUS *lifts the pillow over his head. While he is thus hidden the dream vanishes. It is his bedroom again. He lowers the pillow. Breathing heavily he lifts himself from the side of the bed. An arm shoots out and grabs his ankle. He screams.*

ATHENE	Nasty dream that one.
TELEMACHUS	Get away from me.
ATHENE	You were crying out in your sleep – but you're awake now.
TELEMACHUS	Get out. Get out.
ATHENE	(*Emerges from under the bed. She is disguised as a beggar, a boy, about the same age as* TELEMACHUS.) Ssh – you'll wake the whole house.
TELEMACHUS	Who are you? What are you doing in my bedroom? What are you doing under my bed? Mother!
ATHENE	(*pounces on him and puts her hand across his mouth*) No! Be a good boy now – (*She pulls out a dagger and lets him go.*)
TELEMACHUS	What do you want?
ATHENE	Food. I haven't eaten for three days.
TELEMACHUS	Why not?
ATHENE	Because I've had no food stupid.
TELEMACHUS	Don't call me stupid. I'm not stupid. How did you get in here?
ATHENE	The window.
TELEMACHUS	Are you a murderer?
ATHENE	No.
TELEMACHUS	A thief?
ATHENE	No.
TELEMACHUS	A beggar?
ATHENE	Yes – now get me some food. I beg you.

TELEMACHUS	Beggars don't beg with knives – you're a liar, and a thief. Mother!
ATHENE	(*knocks him down*) Cry out once more and I'll think you're scared of me.
TELEMACHUS	I'm not scared of anything.
ATHENE	Not even dreams?
TELEMACHUS	Dreams are different.
ATHENE	To what?
TELEMACHUS	Get out! Get out! Get out! (*pushes* ATHENE *away*)
ATHENE	I thought the son of Odysseus would have a little more heart, but perhaps I was under the wrong bed. Perhaps you're not his son at all. Let me see – no – you don't remind me of Odysseus one little bit.
TELEMACHUS	Who are you? (*silence*) You've seen my father? Where?
ATHENE	Food first. I'm not used to hunger you see, and it's driving me crazy.
TELEMACHUS	Alright. Wait.
ATHENE	Don't ring the bell – raid the kitchen.
TELEMACHUS	I don't have to raid the kitchen. This is my house.

He rings a small bell – ATHENE *gets under bed again.*

Enter EURYCLEIA.

EURYCLEIA	Yes Master?
TELEMACHUS	Eurycleia. I feel hungry, I'd like some bread. And cheese.
EURYCLEIA	Yes Master. (*She turns away.*)
ATHENE	And pickle.

TELEMACHUS	And – pickle.
EURYCLEIA	Pickle? You don't like pickle.
TELEMACHUS	Well – I'll be adventurous.
EURYCLEIA	You? You alright Master?
TELEMACHUS	Yes I'm fine.
EURYCLEIA	Only you're not very adventurous as a rule.
TELEMACHUS	Please…
EURYCLEIA	A picky little eater …
TELEMACHUS	And hurry.
EURYCLEIA	Very well master. (*She turns to go.*)
ATHENE	And some olives.
EURYCLEIA	Pardon?
TELEMACHUS	Olives.
EURYCLEIA	(*suspicious now*) Anything else?
TELEMACHUS	No – thank you.
ATHENE	(*comes out from under the bed*) So you're a picky little eater?
TELEMACHUS	How do you know my father?
ATHENE	Unadventurous as a rule.
TELEMACHUS	Answer me.

He grabs ATHENE.

ATHENE	Let go. (*He lets go.*) I lent him something once, on the field of battle.
TELEMACHUS	You were at Troy?
ATHENE	Yes. I lent him something and he didn't give it back.

TELEMACHUS	What? What did you lend him?
ATHENE	After the city of Troy fell, its men killed and all the women and children sold into slavery, I stowed away on board your father's ship, thinking I would get my... things back.
TELEMACHUS	What things?
ATHENE	A few miles from the coast of Troy, there was a storm. Plank separated from plank and ditched us all into the sea.
TELEMACHUS	What happened to my father?
EURYCLEIA	(*off*) Master, yer cheese and pickle.

ATHENE *hides under the bed.*

TELEMACHUS	Come in.

Enter EURYCLEIA.

EURYCLEIA	Are you alright Master? I thought I heard voices.
TELEMACHUS	You should see a doctor about that. They can do wonders nowadays.
EURYCLEIA	Don't be cheeky.
TELEMACHUS	I'm sorry.
EURYCLEIA	I'm not in the mood. I'm all nerves. What with yer mother an'all.
TELEMACHUS	What's wrong with her?
EURYCLEIA	And pickles? Not like you at all. And cheese you know will give you bad dreams.

He takes the plate and puts it on the floor. ATHENE'*s hand shoots out and the plate vanishes.*

TELEMACHUS	Well – I – um have had bad dreams. Even tonight I dreamt I saw my father and his friend Achilles – but

they began to fight each other. It was terrible and Achilles was about to kill my father when the vision disappeared and I awoke. What do you think it means?

EURYCLEIA   Nothing. Dreams? Load of rubbish.

The plate has reappeared empty.

You shouldn't eat so fast. Give ee stomach ache.

TELEMACHUS   I was hungry.

She turns to go and then turns back with an anxious look.

EURYCLEIA   Oh master – I'm worried for your mother. All day she sits and spins and all night she unravels every inch. Her mind's disordered and I'm not sure what to do. But you're too young.

TELEMACHUS   Too young? For what?

EURYCLEIA   This house gives me a bad feeling of a sudden, like something dark is about to happen. So be ready Telemachus.

TELEMACHUS   Ready for what?

EURYCLEIA   I feel sure that good times will visit this house again – one day. One day.

ATHENE *belches from under the bed.*

TELEMACHUS   Pickles.

Exit EURYCLEIA.

ATHENE *comes out from under the bed and flops onto it groaning.*

ATHENE   Oh – Oh that hurts most wonderfully.

TELEMACHUS   Get up, get up. What else about my father? Are you telling me you saw him drowned?

ATHENE	No – I saw him floating away on a casque of wine. Clutching my things and grinning like a cat. You must follow him, follow and find him.
TELEMACHUS	Follow where? I can't. I'm…
ATHENE	Too scared?
PENELOPE	(off) Telemachus. Telemachus.
TELEMACHUS	My mother.

ATHENE *gets back under the bed.*

PENELOPE *enters.*

PENELOPE	Eurycleia tells me you've been having bad dreams again.
TELEMACHUS	Yes. I'm alright now.

EURYMACHUS *enters but stands in the shadows unseen. We also are aware of* EURYCLEIA *watching.*

PENELOPE	Would you like me to tell you a story? Jack the giant killer? The witch in the woods?
TELEMACHUS	I'm too old for those stories.
PENELOPE	Too old? (pause) My son, I need to talk to you about Eurymachus.
TELEMACHUS	I don't want to talk about him.
PENELOPE	We must.
TELEMACHUS	Just get rid of him, throw him out.
PENELOPE	I can't, I can't.
TELEMACHUS	Why? (silence) Do you love him?
PENELOPE	No – I fear him, and you must fear him too.
TELEMACHUS	Why did you ever let him stay then? Why did you let him step foot in our house?

PENELOPE   I needed someone. He was there, that's all. Don't think
           badly of me.

TELEMACHUS   But it's father you love – isn't it?

   Silence.

PENELOPE   How can I answer? He's been gone, fourteen years.

TELEMACHUS   But you love him don't you. Don't you?

PENELOPE   Telemachus. We must face the truth now. Either your
           father is dead...

TELEMACHUS   No. No. He's alive. I know it. Don't believe anything
           else, and you'll wait for him won't you? As long as it
           takes, for my sake. Won't you? Won't you?

PENELOPE   Listen to me. Eurymachus wants to be the King of
           Ithaca. To be that he must marry me. He has waited
           and grown sour and mean in waiting. He will wait no
           longer. If I don't agree to marry him, he will kill you. I
           know it, I can see it in his eyes.

   Silence.

TELEMACHUS   If you marry him – I will never speak to you again.

PENELOPE   Telemachus.

TELEMACHUS   Go away. Or promise me, you won't marry him.
           Promise me! Promise me! Promise me!

PENELOPE   I promise.

   Enter EURYMACHUS *with his sword drawn.*

EURYMACHUS   You're a little viper aren't you?

PENELOPE   Eurymachus! Please.

TELEMACHUS   Get out of my room.

EURYMACHUS	I will marry your mother. I will have the palace and the vineyards that once belonged to your father. I will be King of Ithaca. (*He holds the sword to* TELEMACHUS' *throat and stares at* PENELOPE.) Marry me!
TELEMACHUS	You promised. (PENELOPE *drinks from the small bottle given to her by* EURYCLEIA.) Mother? (*She falls.*)
EURYMACHUS	Penelope? Penelope? No – I – wake up. Wake up, I beg you. (*He turns back to* TELEMACHUS *who is too shocked to move.*) This is your fault. You have kept her from her happiness! (*He advances on the boy.*)

Enter EURYCLEIA.

EURYCLEIA	I have seen. I have heard everything.

EURYMACHUS *exits.*

TELEMACHUS	Mother? Mother?
EURYCLEIA	Ssh now. It's alright. It's alright.
TELEMACHUS	Is she dead?
EURYCLEIA	No. She sleeps that's all. A sleep that looks like death.
TELEMACHUS	How? Why?
EURYCLEIA	To save you and herself from Eurymachus. This potion I prepared for her myself – we knew this day would come.
TELEMACHUS	Mother?
EURYCLEIA	She will not wake until I give her the opposing medicine.
TELEMACHUS	Then give it to her now.
EURYCLEIA	No. Eurymachus thinks her dead. Now he will seize the house by force – no one will oppose him. You must escape. Escape.

ATHENE	(*has now come out from under the bed and is watching the scene*) Escape. Find your father, and bring him home. He'll know what to do with Eurymachus.
EURYCLEIA	Who's this?
ATHENE	A friend.
EURYCLEIA	Find your father Telemachus. Go in search of him.
TELEMACHUS	I can't – how?
EURYCLEIA	If you stay, Eurymachus will kill you when my back is turned.
ATHENE	There's a boat in the harbour that sails on the morning tide – we'll stow away.
EURYCLEIA	I'll look after your mother – now go – go.
TELEMACHUS	But – I – I've never been more than a mile from shore.
EURYCLEIA	Have courage – go with your friend – whoever he is. (*He hugs* EURYCLEIA.) And come safely, with your father. Good luck Telemachus son of Odysseus and Penelope. Good luck.

Exit TELEMACHUS *and* ATHENE.

ACT TWO

It's dark. TELEMACHUS *sleeps. As* ATHENE *raises the sails she sings.*
Note: the song should have a wistful air.

ATHENE   Unfurl the sails for the wine dark sea
                Unfurl the sails and set me free
                tomorrow I sail
                tomorrow I'll be
                under the stars
                on the wine dark sea.
                No cross gales, no rocks
                No current I fear
                If the Gods sail with me
                I'll come home my dear
                back to the land
                of my birth one day
                to kiss and make up
                in the time-honoured way.

All exit leaving TELEMACHUS *asleep.*

ATHENE *on watch. We hear the wind. Dawn breaks.*

ATHENE   Telemachus. Wake up now. It's nearly day.

TELEMACHUS   (*half wakes*) I heard singing – singing…

ATHENE   Wake up Telemachus.

She throws some water over him. He stands shocked.

TELEMACHUS   Why's the floor moving? Where am I?

ATHENE   You're at sea. On board a ship.

TELEMACHUS *stares out at the sea.*

TELEMACHUS   The sea? It's a dream – it's a dream ship!

ATHENE	It's no dream.
TELEMACHUS	No? Then where are the sailors? Where's the steersman? Where's the Captain? Ha!
ATHENE	They got off.
TELEMACHUS	Got off?
ATHENE	They went ashore, got drunk and didn't come back. Rather than miss the tide I – I cast off.
TELEMACHUS	You mean…
ATHENE	We drifted out of the harbour, a stiff breeze came by – I unfurled the sails and – away… On the open sea, the wind in our hair. The salt on our skin. Hungry? (*He looks in disdain at the food.*) People on adventures have to eat what they can find. One of the sailors must have left it behind.
TELEMACHUS	(*He won't eat.*) This is – awful – this is – we could get killed – drowned.
ATHENE	You can drown in the bath Telemachus.
TELEMACHUS	I don't want to drown, anywhere. I want to go home. Where are we going? Who sets our course?
ATHENE	Your father.
TELEMACHUS	Why? How? What do you mean?
ATHENE	On the night before the storm which wrecked your father's ship I overheard him talking to his men. He asked them if they would follow him on a great adventure.
TELEMACHUS	Follow him? Where?
ATHENE	West and west again to the edge of the world. 'West and west again,' – those were his words.

TELEMACHUS   But I don't understand, surely he was on his way
               home?

Silence.

               What are you called?

ATHENE   Mentor. At your service master!

TELEMACHUS   You said you gave my father something on the
               battlefield at Troy.

ATHENE   No, I lent him something. It was a loan.

TELEMACHUS   What kind of a loan?

ATHENE   The kind you give back.

TELEMACHUS   Why didn't he?

ATHENE   That I hope to find out.

TELEMACHUS   With my help?

ATHENE   Two heads are better than one, ask any monster. (*She
               dances.*)

He stares out to sea open-mouthed.

TELEMACHUS   Mentor. Mentor!

ATHENE   Where did that come from?

TELEMACHUS   I – it just came out of the water…

ATHENE   A whole island?

TELEMACHUS   We're heading straight for it.

ATHENE   We are – at a rate of knots. Do you know how to
               change course?

TELEMACHUS   Yes but I – I can't do it on my own – it's a combination
               of sails and oars – there isn't time.

They take down the sails.

ATHENE	It just came up – out of the water?
TELEMACHUS	Yes. Yes I told you – we're going to hit it. We're going to hit it smack on.
ATHENE	Maybe we'll hit a beach.
TELEMACHUS	Maybe we'll hit a rock.
ATHENE	Then I suggest we jump overboard and swim for shore. What do you think?
TELEMACHUS	I think I can't swim.
ATHENE	You don't have to swim – just relax, let the waves take you ashore.
TELEMACHUS	Waves? What waves?
ATHENE	Are you ready?
TELEMACHUS	Wait. Wait.
ATHENE	What?
TELEMACHUS	If I should drown, tell my mother. I – I...
ATHENE	Tell her what? What?
TELEMACHUS	That I – I can't think.
ATHENE	You can't think? You can't swim. What are you – a pebble?
TELEMACHUS	Tell her I love her and – and I – wish that...
ATHENE	I understand – are you ready to jump?
TELEMACHUS	Yes.
ATHENE	Steady...
TELEMACHUS	Wait – wait.
ATHENE	For what? We're going to hit the rocks.

TELEMACHUS	Tell my father… if you find him.
ATHENE	What – tell him what? For God's sake.
TELEMACHUS	Tell him I… I… I'm sorry.
ATHENE	Sorry for what?
TELEMACHUS	I don't know – just tell him.
ATHENE	Tell him yourself – are you ready?
TELEMACHUS	No.
ATHENE	Good – Jump! Jump!

There is a climax of sound as they jump into the water. Blackout. The sound of waves gradually takes the place of the sound of the ship hitting the rocks. This becomes a gentle sound, a soft lull of waves and eerie music. When the lights rise again the scene is a plush green tropical island, very mysterious and in total contrast to the colours of Ithaca. TELEMACHUS *and* ATHENE *lie prostrate as if washed up on the beach.* CALYPSO, *the Goddess of the Island, watches them unseen.*

ATHENE	Telemachus? Telemachus?
TELEMACHUS	Am I drowned?
ATHENE	Possibly.
TELEMACHUS	The ship?
ATHENE	Gone. (*She sits up.*)
TELEMACHUS	My clothes, they're dry.
ATHENE	Mine too.
TELEMACHUS	Perhaps then we are drowned. Oh Gods. Are we dead Mentor?
ATHENE	Do you feel dead?

26

TELEMACHUS	No – but then, what place is this if not heaven?
ATHENE	(*to audience*) All about a deep wood grew with summer leaves, alder and black poplar and pungent cypress. Ornate birds here and there rested their stretched wings. The scent of thyme and cedar smoke hung heavy in the air. Four springs of clearest water shallow and clear took channels through lovely beds of violets and tender parsley. Even a God who found this place would gaze and feel her heart beat with delight.
TELEMACHUS	Unless – of course – this is a supernatural place – a place of magic. Hark. Someone is singing? Did you hear? They've stopped now. (*He picks up a stick to defend himself.*) Mentor, someone approaches.
ATHENE	I hear them.
VOICE OF CALYPSO	Who are you? Why have you come to my Island?
ATHENE	Say something.
TELEMACHUS	I am Telemachus, son of the Godlike Hero Odysseus, for whom I search. (*silence*) Where are you? Show yourself. One name deserves another.
ATHENE	Well said master.
TELEMACHUS	Show yourself.

A wolf enters and its growl is full and threatening.

TELEMACHUS	Mentor!

ATHENE	I see it. I see it.
TELEMACHUS	What shall I do?
ATHENE	Ignore it.
TELEMACHUS	What?
ATHENE	Ignore it – it's not there.
TELEMACHUS	But it is there – look – look!
ATHENE	Don't look at it. Don't! It'll take your look as a challenge. Look away. Act superior, feign indifference. It's not a threat. It's nothing. Has it gone yet?
TELEMACHUS	I don't know I'm not looking. (*It growls.*) It's still there. Shall we run?
ATHENE	No! Speak to the voice.
TELEMACHUS	Voice. Is this your creature?
VOICE	Yes. Yes. Yes.
TELEMACHUS	I will kill it with my bare hands if I have to (*pause*) and... and this stick! (*He looks at* MENTOR *and grimaces. She throws him her knife.*) I mean this knife.
CALYPSO	(*laughs*) Oh Telemachus. I am this creature.

He looks at the wolf, which then stands and becomes CALYPSO *the Goddess of the Isle, a mature woman.*

	Welcome Telemachus. Son of Odysseus. And who is this – little one – with the grey eyes?
ATHENE	I am one to be scared of.
CALYPSO	Really.

A net falls onto ATHENE.

ATHENE	Let me go. (*She struggles in vain.*)
TELEMACHUS	Let him go. Let him go – or you'll live to regret it.

CALYPSO	Indeed – one who lives forever as I do lives to regret everything.
TELEMACHUS	Let him go!
CALYPSO	Him? I see no him. I see a her. Tush, tush, have you been keeping secrets little one?
TELEMACHUS	What?
ATHENE	I'm a girl – what difference does it make?
CALYPSO	All the difference in the world my dear.
TELEMACHUS	A girl?
CALYPSO	So upsetting isn't it, when things aren't what they seem? Never fear – I am exactly what I seem.
ATHENE	Exactly.
TELEMACHUS	Who are you?
CALYPSO	I am Calypso, the Goddess of the Isle, which is called Ogygia. How did you come here?
TELEMACHUS	By ship.
CALYPSO	Where is your ship?
TELEMACHUS	On the rocks.
CALYPSO	Oh no – so you're stranded. Tush, tush – What have you done Telemachus – to anger Poseidon the great God of the Sea, that he should try to drown you?
TELEMACHUS	Nothing.
CALYPSO	Something. You must be thirsty – after all that salt he threw at you.
ATHENE	Don't touch the drink.
CALYPSO	And hungry too.
ATHENE	Or the food.

CALYPSO	Do you like pork?
TELEMACHUS	Yes – I –

CALYPSO *points towards* ATHENE *in the net who is transformed into a pig.*

TELEMACHUS	No – No – Mentor. Mentor.
CALYPSO	She understands you. Her flesh is that of a pig but her brain is her own. To be all pig would be no torture at all.
TELEMACHUS	Fiend – demon – witch!
CALYPSO	Your father called me sweeter names by far.
TELEMACHUS	My father? You've seen him?
CALYPSO	Yes. He was here weeping like a child on this very sand. But sand has a way with tears.
TELEMACHUS	When was this?
CALYPSO	Yesterday perhaps, or the year before. I can't remember.
TELEMACHUS	Where did he go? Where is he now?
CALYPSO	Come share my table and I will speak of him.

A table magically appears with food.

TELEMACHUS	Return my servant to his – to her own form and I'll sit with you.
CALYPSO	*Sit!* (*He sits.*) Why do you seek your father?
TELEMACHUS	I... My mother needs him.
CALYPSO	Ah sweet Penelope. He often talked of her. So feminine, so doting, domestic and sacrificial. No wonder he didn't want to go home.

TELEMACHUS	(*stands*) My mother is worth a thousand of you – whoever, whatever you are.
CALYPSO	Forgive me. I forget how high emotions can run in a child. Have something to eat you'll grow more quickly.
TELEMACHUS	I'm not hungry.
CALYPSO	Telemachus. Let us be friends – yes?
TELEMACHUS	My servant.
CALYPSO	Can wait.
TELEMACHUS	How long was my father here?
CALYPSO	Long enough to tire of me, but it wasn't thoughts of home that took him away. It was something else altogether.
TELEMACHUS	What could keep him from our home? Tell me.
CALYPSO	He has a craving to see over the next hill. A restless itch to rove and rummage through the world. A common fault in mortal beings but understandable since mortal beings never know when life will end. I who am immortal have no desire to look over the next hill at all. Perhaps I'm just lazy. Still I enjoyed his stay, and I think he did too.
TELEMACHUS	Why don't you just say it. You and he were…
CALYPSO	Were?
TELEMACHUS	Close.
CALYPSO	As the folded wings of a butterfly. Don't judge him too harshly. He suffered a long hard war, and after all a man alone on an island with an irresistible Goddess… Tea?

He takes some drink.

CALYPSO	Oh Telemachus. I'm so glad you came to visit. I lost a man and found a child.
TELEMACHUS	I'm not a child.
CALYPSO	(*smiles*) I've often wondered what it would be like to be a mother. Is it tremendously hard work do you think?
TELEMACHUS	I don't know.
CALYPSO	No? Still – it would provide one with a purpose I suppose – drink up. (**He drinks more. The drink is lovely.**) Why do you search for your father Telemachus?
TELEMACHUS	I – I told you –
CALYPSO	Do you wish to be like him?
TELEMACHUS	Yes, I think so.
CALYPSO	Then let me be your Tutor, stay with me a little while. The woods will be your playground. The creatures will call you by your name and the streams will flow at your command. (**He is quite drugged by now and she has begun to crawl wolf-like up the table towards him.**) I will give you knowledge you cannot dream of. Stay with me Telemachus and you will never grow old.
TELEMACHUS	(*dreamily*) But I want to grow old – no, no, I want to grow up.
CALYPSO	Up? Up is very overrated. Oh Telemachus it would be such fun to have a child around the place.
TELEMACHUS	I'm not a child.
CALYPSO	A boy, a youth.
TELEMACHUS	What have you done?
CALYPSO	Ssh. (**She strokes him – he is drugged.**) Why do you search for your father?

TELEMACHUS	I – I told you –
CALYPSO	Tush, tush – tell me the truth.
TELEMACHUS	Where are you?
CALYPSO	I'm here – inside your dreams. Telemachus.
HELPERS	Telemachus.
TELEMACHUS	Mother? Is that you?
CALYPSO	My son – don't leave me.
TELEMACHUS	I must – I
CALYPSO	Please don't leave me here, all alone.
TELEMACHUS	But I have to go.
CALYPSO	Your father has gone to the edge of the world.
HELPERS	Too far – too far.
TELEMACHUS	I'll bring him home, I promised.
CALYPSO	You're so scared, so frightened.
TELEMACHUS	Yes.
CALYPSO	Don't leave me then – stay.
TELEMACHUS	No.
CALYPSO	Tush tush – don't you love me Telemachus?
TELEMACHUS	Yes. Yes.
CALYPSO	If you love me, stay with me. Don't desert me as your father did. You're not like him, are you? Stay and be my son – for ever.
TELEMACHUS	Mentor!
CALYPSO	Ssh. I will comfort you as I did when you were a child.
CAST	Give up your search.

CALYPSO	My son.
CALYPSO/ HELPERS	The woods will be your playground. The creatures will call you by name. The streams will flow at your command.
CALYPSO	My son.
TELEMACHUS	Yes. Yes. Yes.
CALYPSO	Yes – Oh Telemachus – welcome – it will be so nice to have your company. (*A momentous hush. The* HELPERS *gaze on expectantly.*) One kiss from my lips and you will be young – forever. (*She bends to kiss him. He stabs her. She howls.* TELEMACHUS *slumps to his knees. We hear whispered voices saying: 'My son, my son' – and he faints.*)

Lights fade to darkness as the beautiful music of the island returns. The lights slowly rise as if the dawn is breaking. The dense suffocation of the previous dark scene is now beautifully contrasted. TELEMACHUS *and* ATHENE, *no longer a pig, lie sleeping.* TELEMACHUS *wakes clutching his head.*

TELEMACHUS	Oh – I'll never drink again – Mentor?
ATHENE	(*wakes with a start*) Ah! What am I?
TELEMACHUS	Yourself.
ATHENE	God of Gods – I thank you. Where is she?
TELEMACHUS	I don't know.
ATHENE	(*shudders*) To be human is bad enough, but to be a human inside a pig is – disgusting. What happened?
TELEMACHUS	I'm not sure – I had a terrifying dream.
ATHENE	I told you not to drink that stuff.
TELEMACHUS	I remember now – I think – I killed her. (*He hears the voice of* CALYPSO *laughing.*) Where are you?

After a moment Calypso *enters carrying some gifts of food and drink.*

Calypso	Good morning.
Telemachus	What do you want?
Calypso	To say goodbye.
Telemachus	We can go?
Calypso	Of course. You made your decision last night. (*She brings out a magnificent golden sword.*) It seems I cannot keep you here, any more than your father. Heaven knows I tried. This was his sword. It's yours now.
Telemachus	My father's?
Calypso	Yes.
Telemachus	(*He does not take the sword.*) He left it here.
Calypso	All the gentlemen who come here leave their swords, so that I may remember them. I've quite a collection, all shapes and sizes.
Telemachus	My father is a soldier. He wouldn't leave his sword. You've killed him haven't you, with your magic, like you tried to kill me?
Calypso	Take the sword.
Telemachus	No.
Calypso	Please, do not upset me.
Athene	Take the sword Telemachus.
Telemachus	She tried to kill me.
Athene	(*pulls him to one side*) If she wanted to kill you – you'd be dead. Take the sword. (*He pulls away.*) You cannot refuse the gift of a Goddess.

TELEMACHUS   My father –

ATHENE   Your father lives, and that's his sword. Believe me – I know. This was the sword he used in the final battle at Troy. I saw him. Take it or I will take it.

TELEMACHUS   (*takes his sword*) How will you remember my father?

CALYPSO   (*laughs*) Oh you're so young. Here's some food for your journey and the raft is yours.

TELEMACHUS   It hardly looks safe.

CALYPSO   It's like the one your father left in. He built his own.

TELEMACHUS   I can build a raft as well as he.

CALYPSO   Beware of Poseidon – if the God of the Sea is angry with you – he will ditch you into the deep no matter what craft you sail in.

TELEMACHUS   We're safe then, because I have done nothing to anger the God of the Sea.

CALYPSO   Not you perhaps – but your father? I have prepared this for you. If you are thrown into the sea, drink it – it will give you the strength to reach land.

TELEMACHUS   Thank you.

CALYPSO   Oh Telemachus – you have turned your back on a long and luxurious life. For what? To follow the wake of your father's ship? Be careful where it leads.

ATHENE *and* TELEMACHUS *get on the raft.*

Farewell Telemachus, Son of Odysseus and Penelope.

Music and lights change. The raft is at sea.

ATHENE   The Goddess conjured a warm land breeze to blow and with joy Telemachus shook out the sail glad to be on his way. He leant on the oar

steering night after night, unsleeping,
watching the stars.
He drank a dusky wine
which the beautiful Calypso had given him
and for seventeen days and nights he sailed
away from the island of Ogygia,
West and West again –
following his father
To the Edge of the World.

Music – TELEMACHUS *and* ATHENE *both sleep.*

CAST   (*sing*) Telemachus, Telemachus
                On the wine dark sea
                Sailing westward,
                Ever westward.
                To the Edge of the World.
                Telemachus, Telemachus…

TELEMACHUS *dreams:* ODYSSEUS *and* ACHILLES *enter as in Act One,
and repeat their fight sequence.* TELEMACHUS *turns in his sleep,
murmurs 'Stop-stop'. As before the fight reaches a climax
where* ODYSSEUS *falls and* ACHILLES *raises the spear for the kill.*

TELEMACHUS   No! (*wakes*)

ATHENE   (*wakes*) Ah!

*The dream/vision fades. She jumps up with a start, nearly falls
in the sea. He catches her, stands for a second holding her,
then lets go.*

ATHENE   Another dream? (TELEMACHUS *nods.*) As before?

TELEMACHUS   Yes, but it makes no sense.

ATHENE   It's a dream. That's all –

TELEMACHUS   But my father and Achilles were great friends. Why
               should they fight?

ATHENE	(*hands him some food*) Here. Eat more, dream less.
TELEMACHUS	I'm not hungry.
ATHENE	As far as I've observed, half the joy of being human is in the eating. (*She eats merrily, while Telemachus stares out to sea with a fixed expression.*) What now?
TELEMACHUS	You should have told me.
ATHENE	Why does it bother you? Half the world is female you know.
TELEMACHUS	Friends should be honest with one another that's all.
ATHENE	Are we friends?
TELEMACHUS	What could you – a girl – have given my father on the battlefield of Troy? What were you doing there in the first place? What are you doing here on a raft on the open sea – with me?
ATHENE	You really are a picky eater.
TELEMACHUS	Tell me the truth! Who are you?
ATHENE	Mentis is the female version of Mentor.
TELEMACHUS	Mentis?
ATHENE	Call me Mentis.
TELEMACHUS	Why can't you tell me your real name? Why are you so secretive?
ATHENE	When you find your father, I will get my real name back – along with the rest of my things. Until then my real name is lost to me – and to you.
TELEMACHUS	Why do you need me to get your things back? Why didn't you just go off and find my father on your own?

ATHENE	I have a father too you know, and he told me to find you and urge you on your journey and for me to go with you. It's my punishment.
TELEMACHUS	Being with me is your punishment?
ATHENE	In a way.
TELEMACHUS	For what?
ATHENE	The things I lent your father on the battlefield of Troy were originally a gift from my father to me.
TELEMACHUS	And he was angry when you gave –
ATHENE	Lent.
TELEMACHUS	When you lent these things to my father. (**ATHENE** *nods*.) So then. Who is *your* father?
ATHENE	Before you can open the gate Telemachus, you have to walk down the path –
TELEMACHUS	You are infuriating.
ATHENE	I know. I know. You really should eat something.
TELEMACHUS	I'm not hungry. (*silence*)
ATHENE	Telemachus?
TELEMACHUS	What?
ATHENE	Have you ever kissed a girl? (*He looks at his feet.*) I said…
TELEMACHUS	I know.
ATHENE	Well?
TELEMACHUS	It's none of your business.

She stands. As this is going on, an image of Poseidon appears, large and dominating, as if rising out of the water behind them – they continue oblivious.

What are you doing?

ATHENE You don't have to kiss me if you don't want to. Do you want to?

TELEMACHUS (*shakes his head*) Yes.

ATHENE Are you sure?

TELEMACHUS It's just that – I wasn't expecting this – on a raft.

ATHENE It's alright – no-one's looking.

By this time the image of Poseidon looms over them. As they are about to kiss, he lets out a thunderous roar. They turn, see him and scream.

ATHENE Poseidon!

The raft is split in two – and ATHENE *and* TELEMACHUS *drift apart. Thunder and lightning.*

ATHENE The potion, drink the potion – she gave you.

TELEMACHUS I can't find it.

ATHENE (*It's on her side of the raft.*) I've got it – I've got it.

TELEMACHUS You drink it – it'll give you the strength to reach land.

ATHENE No – you drink it. (*She throws it across the sea to him. He drinks it.*)

The stage goes dark. MENTIS *has gone. The sound reaches its climax.*

TELEMACHUS Mentis – Mentis – Mentis… (*His voice trails away.*)

Blackout.

ACT THREE

Nausicaa.

Lights rise. The stage is empty but for a bush behind which Telemachus *hides, because he's naked. He had been washed ashore on the Island of Phaecia where* Alcinous *is King and* Arete, *his wife, Queen. Their daughter* Nausicaa *now enters with her brother* Laodomus.

Laodomus	We ought to be getting back.
Nausicaa	Why? – it's the best part of the day. Here catch. (*She throws a ball to her brother.*)
Laodomus	Nausicaa.
Nausicaa	Well come on – throw it back.
Laodomus	We're not children anymore. (*He puts the ball down.*)
Nausicaa	No.
Laodomus	Let's make a move.
Nausicaa	What's the matter, are you bored?
Laodomus	I don't like coming here – and you know why.
Nausicaa	Well I do.
Laodomus	Forget him Sister.
Nausicaa	Have you forgotten him?
Laodomus	I'm going home.
Nausicaa	Perhaps if I sit here for a while the sea breeze will blow him from my mind.

LAODOMUS	Nausicaa. Look what I've found. (*He picks up* TELEMACHUS' *trousers which have been washed ashore.*) And here's something else. (TELEMACHUS' *shirt.*) You shouldn't stay here on your own.
NAUSICAA	Don't worry so much – they're just rags. You go back Laodomus. I'll follow in a little while.
LAODOMUS	It's getting cold. (*He leaves her his cloak.*)
NAUSICAA	You're such a gentleman these days. Whatever happened to my horrid brother?
LAODOMUS	(*throws the trousers and shirt at her*) He's still here. (*laughs*) Don't be long.

He exits.

NAUSICAA	(*sings*) As I was out walking one morning in May I saw a young sailor and this he did say Come to me now and be my dear wife an' I'll love you truly, all of my life.
TELEMACHUS	(*as she finishes the song, he looks up from behind the bush*) Excuse me.
NAUSICAA	Laodomus, Laodomus.
TELEMACHUS	Please – don't be frightened, I mean you no harm.
NAUSICAA	Who are you? Why are you spying on me?
TELEMACHUS	I'm not, I'm not.
NAUSICAA	Then why are you hiding behind that bush?
TELEMACHUS	This isn't what it looks like.
NAUSICAA	No?
TELEMACHUS	I'm not spying on you. I've been shipwrecked.
NAUSICAA	There are no signs here of a shipwreck.

TELEMACHUS	It was a small craft – broken in two by the great God of the Sea. It's probably been washed up on another part of the island. Is this an island?
NAUSICAA	What are you hiding behind there?
TELEMACHUS	Nothing – whatsoever.
NAUSICAA	Then come out – with your hands up.
TELEMACHUS	Um … (*He raises one hand.*) Wait one moment. (*He breaks off a branch and then emerges with the branch strategically placed.*) I – I wasn't spying – honestly.
NAUSICAA	What happened to your clothes?
TELEMACHUS	I – I took them off when I fell into the sea, fearing that they would drag me under. I swam for many hours – and thought I would drown but then I saw the outline of these hills. By the time I reached the safety of this sand I was exhausted and lay down to sleep. I awoke when I heard you singing. I need help.

Enter ATHENE *carrying his sword.*

ATHENE	Telemachus. You're alive – and – naked. (*She sees* NAUSICAA.) Ah.
NAUSICAA	And this is?
TELEMACHUS	My servant – Mentis?
NAUSICAA	I am Nausicaa. My father is the King of this land, which is called Phaecia. The Gods deal out fortune to good and bad men as they please. They have sent you hardship and you must bear it, but now that you have taken refuge here you shall not lack clothing or any other comfort due to a poor man in distress. Yours? (*She gives him his trousers and shirt, turns away as he dresses.*)
TELEMACHUS	What do you think?

ATHENE	Of what?
TELEMACHUS	The princess. She's a Princess.
ATHENE	(*sarcastic*) How are you Mentis? I'm so glad to see you alive. I feared you were drowned, and I wept all night but when I discovered you were still alive my heart danced with joy!
TELEMACHUS	She's beautiful don't you think? Mentis?
ATHENE	You look ridiculous.

NAUSICAA *turns and laughs.*

TELEMACHUS	My name is Telemachus.
NAUSICAA	You may present your petition to my father.

Music. A fanfare. Enter ALCINOUS, *King of the Phaecians and his Queen* ARETE, *and their son* LAODOMUS. *The palace.*

ALCINOUS	Rise stranger. Tell us how you came to my kingdom and how I may help you. We are a generous people.
TELEMACHUS	My name is Telemachus. I arrived here by the hand of the great Earthshaker Poseidon – who – you see I was given this raft.
ATHENE	Stick to the point.
TELEMACHUS	By the Goddess Calypso, who's a wolf actually, on the Island of Ogygia, and she gave me this sword too.
ATHENE	Don't waffle.
TELEMACHUS	Poseidon snapped our raft in two like you would a biscuit and I swam ashore as did my servant, who's a girl, actually. (ALCINOUS *and* ARETE *exchange glances.*) And there I met your daughter, Nausicaa – who (*pause*) you see I'm searching for my father.
ALCINOUS	Ah!

TELEMACHUS	He's been missing many years and I must find him because an evil man called Eurymachus has taken control of his house, lands and wealth, and I was too young to stop him.
ALCINOUS	What is your father's name?
TELEMACHUS	Proudly may I say it and proud I am to be his son for he is a hero of the Trojan War, the Godlike Odysseus.

ALCINOUS's *expression darkens, he rises.*

LAODOMUS	Odysseus!

ALCINOUS *draws a sword and approaches* TELEMACHUS. *He puts his sword to the boy's throat.*

ARETE	No.
NAUSICAA	No.
ATHENE	No.
ALCINOUS	I would kill you now but for the sound of women's voices, son of Odysseus.
TELEMACHUS	(*Much to everyone's surprise, he beats back* ALCINOUS's *sword with his own.*) Your daughter led me to believe you were a civilised people.
ARETE	We are. (*firmly to her husband*) We are! (*He returns to her side.*) No sword will leave its scabbard in this chamber. (*silence*) When did you last see your father Telemachus?
TELEMACHUS	I've never seen him, except in my dreams. He left for the war when I was an infant.
ARETE	How do you know then, that he is a hero?

TELEMACHUS	By reputation, who has not heard how he fought back to back with the great Achilles against a hundred Trojan Warriors? Who has not heard the story of the Wooden Horse?
LAODOMUS	We heard it – many times – from his own lips.
TELEMACHUS	He is a soldier beyond compare.
ARETE	We are a sea-faring people Telemachus. Our ships are blessed by the Gods. We love the sports, singing, dancing and the pleasures of our beds. We do not honour soldiers, as other Kingdoms do. War brings out the beast in men, it makes them liars and cheats. In the case of your father it made him a very good one. He lied to us. He cheated us.
TELEMACHUS	It is not so. It is not so.

Silence.

ALCINOUS	Your father was shipwrecked on our shore. My daughter found him as she found you, naked and lonely and afraid, although he would not show it. He was older, mature and handsome. A man of the world who spoke sweetly and with confidence. He swiftly saw the admiration in her eyes. He did not say at first who he was or that he was married. Instead he let her fall in love with him, a girl, who's heart was open, tender and easy to abuse. We fed and clothed him, gave him a royal bed to sleep in. I gave him my own golden cup to drink from, and a ship that could sail the sea sightless, with no need of a steersman, a ship blessed by the Gods which always came home to harbour. These things I gave because I thought, as my daughter thought, that at last the sea had brought our royal house a worthy husband. But in his heart he had no love for her and no intention of staying. When he had procured from us all his needs he told her he

46

was married, with a son. We did not expect to meet
you Telemachus. My daughter loved him, and kept
his departure secret from us. He sailed away under
cover of night, like a thief, taking with him twenty of
our sailors whom he had bribed with honey-tongued
tales of glory and adventure. (*pause*) He sailed West,
leaving behind him grief and bitterness and a young
girl's broken heart. (TELEMACHUS *weeps*.) Tears become
a man Telemachus, but we trust them less today then
yesterday. Your father was a copious weeper. We will
provide you with shelter and food, and I will decide
your fate in the morning.

Exit all but ATHENE *and* TELEMACHUS.

ATHENE	Telemachus.
TELEMACHUS	Leave me alone.
ATHENE	Yes Master.
TELEMACHUS	How could he behave like that? He couldn't have, he just wouldn't.
ATHENE	But he did.
TELEMACHUS	Why?

Enter NAUSICAA.

ATHENE	Send her away. If her father finds her here, he will kill you.
NAUSICAA	My father is asleep.
ATHENE	Telemachus…
TELEMACHUS	Be still Mentis, you'll wake the whole house. Keep watch a while.
ATHENE	No. The answer is no.

TELEMACHUS	If her father finds her here, he will probably kill both of us, so for your own sake, keep the watch – please.
ATHENE	This is against my better judgement. Not that it matters – I'm just a servant. (*She keeps watch.*)
TELEMACHUS	Is it true what they said about my father?
NAUSICAA	Yes.
TELEMACHUS	I'm sorry.
NAUSICAA	Why should you be sorry? You've done nothing wrong.
TELEMACHUS	Why did you come?
NAUSICAA	To give you this. (*She gives him a shield of gold.* ATHENE *sees this – it is her shield.*) Your father gave it me, as a present. He said he won it on the battlefield of Troy. It's yours.
TELEMACHUS	But he gave it to you.
NAUSICAA	I don't want it. I don't need it –
TELEMACHUS	It's solid gold.
NAUSICAA	(*smiles*) My 'young heart' isn't as fragile as my father thinks. Please don't think too badly of my father. He's upset, as you could see. (*laughs*) He feels he was made a fool of. His pride was hurt. My mother will talk to him and by the morning he'll be calmer. (*silence*) You're very young to undertake a voyage such as yours.
TELEMACHUS	I had no choice.
NAUSICAA	Your father told me he came from an island called Ithaca.
TELEMACHUS	Yes.
NAUSICAA	When he spoke of it he wept.
TELEMACHUS	Then why doesn't he come home?

Silence.

NAUSICAA   Tell me about this 'Ithaca'.

TELEMACHUS   Ithaca? It's dryer than here, dusty, rocky, but it has – a sparse beauty and if you know where to look there are small lush valleys with silver streams. There are thousands of olive trees and all kinds of places in which to – to play.

NAUSICAA   And you live in a large house?

TELEMACHUS   A palace, with great oak doors which my father carved with his own hands before I was born. It seems so far away now – like a dream.

NAUSICAA   I've never been anywhere. I'm not allowed to leave the island. (*silence*) And your father was so 'travelled'. I have no regrets Telemachus, none, and as for my father, his anger is his own.

TELEMACHUS   Nausicaa, when my father left the island did he say where he was going?

NAUSICAA   West, and west again.

TELEMACHUS   And what lies to the West of here?

NAUSICAA   The land of the Cyclops – but do not go near them. They are a race of Giants who if our sailors are to be believed are cruel beyond imagination. I must go. Good luck Telemachus.

TELEMACHUS   Nausicaa –

She has gone. He picks up the shield. He matches it up with the sword, then rests.

ATHENE   Night fell over the palace and Telemachus
watchful and full of feeling
gazed on its beauty.
Four spacious orchards surrounded the court,

with trees in bloom
or weighted down for picking.
Luscious figs and olives ripe and dark.
Fruit never failed upon their boughs.
The breathing west wind ripened all in turn.
This was the gift from heaven
to Arete and Alcinous.
But through these pleasant grounds
stalked a prince with murder in his heart
for Telemachus.

Master, Master. Wake up. Someone's coming, stealthily.

TELEMACHUS   Who?

ATHENE   The brother of your girlfriend.

Enter LAODOMUS *armed.*

TELEMACHUS   Laodomus. Why have you come?

LAODOMUS   Pick up your sword. (*silence*) If you refuse my challenge I will run you through for cowardice. Pick up your sword.

TELEMACHUS   Why do you wish to fight me?

LAODOMUS   You are your father's son.

TELEMACHUS   But not him. I am not him.

LAODOMUS   How quick you are to disclaim him now. Now fight. (*He lunges at* TELEMACHUS *who jumps aside.*)

ATHENE   Pick up the sword. Pick it up. (TELEMACHUS *does so.*)

LAODOMUS   Your father was a great fighter – or so he told me. (*He attacks* TELEMACHUS *who defends himself but does not fight back.*)

TELEMACHUS   I urge you to follow your father's example and stay your sword before one of us is killed.

LAODOMUS *attacks him again.*

ATHENE   Fight back you fool – fight back.

LAODOMUS *attacks him again and still Telemachus parries and retreats.*

TELEMACHUS   Then think of your sister. How will she feel, kneeling at the side of your grave?

LAODOMUS   *(attacks him more strongly now and pins* TELEMACHUS *down)* My sister? I saw her come here. Did you think to make fools of us a second time? *(He raises his sword to kill* TELEMACHUS *but* ATHENE *cries out.)*

ATHENE   No! *(leaps on his back)*

He throws her down and brings his sword upon her. His sword is about to strike her when TELEMACHUS *blocks it with his own.*

TELEMACHUS   Once again. Lay down your sword.

LAODOMUS   *(Now full of rage, he beats* TELEMACHUS *back again, knocking the sword from his hand.)* Whose grave do you see now, Telemachus?

ATHENE   Murder! Murder! Ring the alarm. Murder.

A bell rings. TELEMACHUS *uses the shield to ward off the blows. King* ALCINOUS *and Queen* ARETE *enter as* LAODOMUS *is about to strike the final blow.*

ALCINOUS   Hold – Hold Laodomus!

ARETE   Laodomus, lay down your sword.

ALCINOUS   Lay it down.

LAODOMUS   But father...

ALCINOUS   Get out. Get out – out!

Enter NAUSICAA.

NAUSICAA   Who rang the bell? Laodomus?

Exit LAODOMUS.

                Telemachus. He's bleeding.

ALCINOUS   Stay away from him.

NAUSICAA   But father…

ALCINOUS   Will no-one do as I say?

ARETE   Nausicaa. Stand by me.

ALCINOUS   Are you badly hurt?

TELEMACHUS   No.

ALCINOUS   The dawn is almost here, there's no need now to delay. You're free to leave my Kingdom. Your craft has been washed ashore. My shipwrights will repair it.

NAUSICAA   Will you give him a proper ship?

ALCINOUS   I will give him his life.

NAUSICAA   He'll perish on the sea, or the current will draw him to the land of the Cyclops. Is that how merciful you are?

Silence.

ALCINOUS   Of all our sailors bribed by Odysseus only one has returned, one. He says that Odysseus visited the land of the Cyclops, for what reason I cannot tell, only the result, all those men, who were my subjects are dead. (*pause*) If you wish to find your father, go to the land of the Cyclops.

ARETE   Telemachus – forgive my son. On many firelit nights your father filled his head with Tales of Troy, great battles and deeds of blood. How easily the seeds of war are sown in a young man, despite all our care. He promised to take Laodomus with him on his adventures, but when the day came he left him behind, and my son's heart hardened against him. But I am grateful – for if my son had gone... Farewell Telemachus. May the Gods be kind to you.

TELEMACHUS   And to your house.

Exit Queen ARETE.

NAUSICAA   I beg you – give up your search. Go home Telemachus.

TELEMACHUS   I've come too far.

NAUSICAA   Then avoid the Cyclops.

TELEMACHUS   But my father.

NAUSICAA   If your father went there he is dead, and a Cyclops is gnawing on his bones.

TELEMACHUS   What do you mean?

NAUSICAA   The Giants of the land feed on people. Go home Telemachus. Go home.

TELEMACHUS   Tell your father not to be too hard on Laodomus. Farewell Nausicaa.

NAUSICAA   Farewell stranger. In your land, if you ever see it again, remember me who found you and offered you the hospitality of my home – and heart.

TELEMACHUS   (*kneels*) Daughter of the Great Alcinous and Arete, Nausicaa. May Zeus the Lord of Thunder grant me daybreak in my own country and all my days until I die I will invoke you as I would a Goddess – Princess, to whom I owe my life.

Exit NAUSICAA.

ATHENE   Spoken like a man.

TELEMACHUS   Laodomus could have killed me – why did you leave it so long – why didn't you ring the bell...?

ATHENE   I'm sorry – I simply assumed that you were the hero of this adventure.

TELEMACHUS   Very funny.

A light rises on the raft.

ATHENE   See, our old friend is here again.

MENTIS   The King is true to his word. Come, lend me a hand.

They pull the craft downstage. As they do the lights change. We hear the sound of the seas, and in the distance we see NAUSICAA *waving farewell.*

TELEMACHUS   Farewell Nausicaa.

ACT FOUR

TELEMACHUS *and* ATHENE *alone on the raft far out at sea heading west.*

CAST	(*sing*) Telemachus, Telemachus Will you see your home again The land you love the best Is no more than a dream ITHACA
ATHENE	(*speaks over the music*) Oh Zeus God of Gods. Look down upon this boy as he sails ever westward to the edge of the world. Why do you cry Telemachus? (*pause*) You have to admit your father is a resourceful man, like yourself.
TELEMACHUS	I'm not like him and don't ever say it again. I should never have left home.
ATHENE	Eurymachus would have killed you.
TELEMACHUS	This trip will kill me.
ATHENE	It hasn't yet.
TELEMACHUS	Have you no fear Mentis?
ATHENE	Fear? Yes, but I've discovered that fear is nothing to be afraid of. It protects you, stops you making foolish errors. Fear is a friend.
TELEMACHUS	Not to me. All my life I've been afraid. Afraid of other children, afraid of Eurymachus, afraid my mother would forget my father, afraid he would never come back. Right now I'm more afraid then ever. All those fears are nothing in comparison to this.
ATHENE	You're scared of the Giant.

55

TELEMACHUS Of course I'm scared of the Giant. He eats people. I'm a boy. This is ridiculous, the whole thing's got out of hand. How may I defend myself – against such an Ogre?

ATHENE You have your sword, your shield.

TELEMACHUS A great help. I couldn't even defeat Laodomus, a boy my own age. (*silence*) And if I ever found my father, what then? Does he want me to find him? I don't think so. I want to go home Mentis.

ATHENE Me too. I have a lovely home, high in the mountains, where the air is thin and clear. You can see the whole world from up there. I'd turn the boat around and head east if I could. But I can't – until I find…

TELEMACHUS Don't talk to me about your things. I don't care a jot about your mysterious 'things' if you won't tell me what they are, they don't exist. (*silence*) I used to lie on my bed and dream of the day I would leave home. I imagined a life at sea, but not like this. The sea seems drier and more desolate than my own Ithaca. If I close my eyes I can see the colours of the Isle. I can smell the thyme on the mountainside. I can hear the grasshoppers singing in the evening and the bells of the goats ringing in the morning as they move down the slopes through the olive groves.

CAST (*sing*) ITHACA

ATHENE Westward we sailed towards the setting sun.
On the evening of the third day we arrived
at the Kingdom of the Cyclops
and high in cliffs we saw the mouth
of his cave. It was a blackhole from out
of which drifted a vile, foreboding stench.

They leave the raft and are outside the cave of the CYCLOPS. *We hear the sound of hammer on anvil. It gets louder then stops.*

TELEMACHUS   What sounds are these?

ATHENE   Where are you going? (*pulls him back*)

TELEMACHUS   Are you afraid?

ATHENE   Of course I'm afraid. He eats people.

TELEMACHUS   What happened to your curiosity? Your love of adventure?

ATHENE   Perhaps we should hide, survey the creature from a distance.

TELEMACHUS   If I hide, I'll have time to think. If I have time to think I'll be overcome with dread. Come let's speak with him and be gone.

ATHENE   Wait! Wait! Why this sudden impetuousness. Speak with him by all means, but try not to be so…

TELEMACHUS   So?

ATHENE   Honest. Don't be so ready to tell him who you really are – it gets us into trouble.

TELEMACHUS   I'm not a good liar.

ATHENE   Poor liars make good meals.

Lights now reveal the back of the cave and we see the giant as a huge blacksmith. His one eye is now sightless. He fumbles round his cave for his tools. He curses under his breath. He then stops and smells the scent of TELEMACHUS.

CYCLOPS   Who's there? I will find you wherever you are. I can smell the sweat on your skin, the sea in your hair, the food on your breath. Speak to me. (*He picks up one of his blacksmiths' tools which becomes a weapon.*) Who's there?

TELEMACHUS	A friend.
CYCLOPS	I have no friends. What friends I had – I had for dinner. (*He takes a lunge for* TELEMACHUS *who leaps aside.*)
TELEMACHUS	I mean you no harm Cyclops.
CYCLOPS	(*throws back his head and laughs a huge resounding laugh*) What harm can you do me? Your throat is no wider than a reed pipe, your voice no deeper than a song bird.

TELEMACHUS *turns to* ATHENE *and she shakes her head and puts her finger to her lips.*

TELEMACHUS	(*mouths*) He's blind.
CYCLOPS	Are you alone – little one? (*silence*) Since I lost my sight my sense of smell has increased tenfold – but yet though I sense another, I smell only one.
TELEMACHUS	I'm not alone. I have a whole crew of sailors waiting on the beach, who will come and slay you if I don't return by nightfall.
CYCLOPS	Poor little songbird, you cannot even lie with conviction. (*He makes another grab for* TELEMACHUS. TELEMACHUS *drops his sword – the giant picks it up.*) What do you want of Polyphemus? Have you come to kill me? Tell me the truth.
TELEMACHUS	I'm looking for someone.
CYCLOPS	You are fortunate to have eyes – I am not so lucky. (*He makes another grab for* TELEMACHUS *who again avoids him.*) Whom do you seek?
TELEMACHUS	Odysseus. The Hero of Troy.
CYCLOPS	Odysseus. What is he – to you?
TELEMACHUS	My – my enemy.

CYCLOPS	Why do you seek him?
TELEMACHUS	To kill him.

The giant suddenly loses his temper and roars 'Odysseus!' He picks up a sack and turns it upside down and out falls a pile of bloody bones. He picks up a bone and still raging he swipes at the air till he rests.

TELEMACHUS	(*gently*) Odysseus. Has he been here? Are his bones among these?
CYCLOPS	Give me your name.
TELEMACHUS	I am… My name is…
CYCLOPS	Tell me the truth

ATHENE *shakes her head.*

TELEMACHUS	I am Telemachus. The son of Odysseus.
CYCLOPS	(*laughs again*) His son. His son. Ah the Gods are kind to me. They weep for the lost eye of Polyphemus. You are their gift to me, and I give thanks.
TELEMACHUS	Where is my father?
CYCLOPS	Gone! (*silence*) Why did he come here Telemachus? What was I to him? A curiosity – nothing more. These are the bones of his men. Nineteen Phaecian sailors – whom he brought with him. I ate them all but one, who escaped with your father.
TELEMACHUS	He lives then.
CYCLOPS	He lives, he speaks, he hears, he sees. (*He makes another grab for* **TELEMACHUS** *who again avoids him – just.*) If he were here, I would make him suffer as he made me suffer, as I will make you suffer. I will catch you Telemachus, and with burning spikes I will gouge out your eyes and your screams will be music to my soul!

TELEMACHUS	He did that to you?
CYCLOPS	He blinded me. He burnt out my eye. My screams reached the heavens, and Poseidon, my uncle, heard me, and has brought you to me – for my sweet revenge. (*He takes another lunge for* TELEMACHUS *and catches him.*) Now Telemachus, what say you?
TELEMACHUS	Let me go Polyphemus, and I will find my father and kill him – will that not be revenge enough?
CYCLOPS	You are a trickster too – just like your father.
TELEMACHUS	It's the truth – I hate my father.
CYCLOPS	It's a lie – you do not hate your father enough to kill him.
TELEMACHUS	I do – I do.
CYCLOPS	Say it then. Say it. Say it!
TELEMACHUS	I hate my father, I hate my father.
CYCLOPS	Oh. (*sadly*) There is such sad conviction now in your voice Telemachus. But you do not hate as I hate. I hate him with all the strength of all the armies of the world. I hate him with all the burning power of my pain – my eye. He has taken from me all the pretty things – all the flowers that I loved to see each season. Now the natural world is as dark as my smithy. For what. Why? Why?
TELEMACHUS	You destroyed the lives of his crew, you devoured their flesh.
CYCLOPS	But that, my boy, is my nature. All who come here, know this. It doesn't mean I'm bad. I did not deserve this dark world Telemachus. I am innocent, as you are. But innocence does not save us. It will not save you. (*He opens his jaws.*)

TELEMACHUS   Mentis.

MENTIS gives him his sword – he plunges it into the giant who roars and falls back clutching his heart.

CYCLOPS   Who? Who gave you the blade?

TELEMACHUS   My servant.

CYCLOPS   Servant? I could smell no-one. (*He breathes heavily.*) You have killed me. Telemachus. You have killed me. You are kinder than your father.

TELEMACHUS   Where is he? Where did he go?

CYCLOPS   West to the edge of the world, beyond which there is nothing, only, only the halls of the dead, where I am bound – where you have sent me – Telemachus, Son of Odysseus. (*He dies.*)

ATHENE   Come. Come. We must go.

They retreat back into the light. The cave darkens and disappears from view.

ATHENE   Come on Telemachus.

TELEMACHUS   I never meant to kill him.

ATHENE   What choice did he give you? You have to hurry. Your father isn't far ahead. (*She pushes him towards the raft.*)

TELEMACHUS   What? What are you doing?

ATHENE   Your father has gone to the halls of the dead.

TELEMACHUS   I don't care. I do not care.

ATHENE   To get there it seems –

TELEMACHUS   I no longer wish to find my father. Therefore I have no reason to continue this journey.

Silence.

ATHENE What about me?

TELEMACHUS You. Ha. (*to her face*) Ha!

ATHENE But don't you care about me?

TELEMACHUS I wish I were dead!

Silence.

ATHENE I beg you. Continue the search for your father.

TELEMACHUS Tell me who you are. Why couldn't the Cyclops smell you?

ATHENE I will tell you everything soon...

TELEMACHUS Hah!

ATHENE And I will reward you.

TELEMACHUS You, oh nice! What could you give me that I would possibly want?

ATHENE Friendship. Self-belief... Some rope.

TELEMACHUS Do you realise where we are?

ATHENE I believe, we've reached the edge of the world.

TELEMACHUS The edge of the world?

ATHENE If your father survived it, so can you.

TELEMACHUS Don't – just don't.

ATHENE I'm sorry.

TELEMACHUS Just tell me – what the rope is for?

ATHENE The rope?

TELEMACHUS The rope Mentis!

ATHENE I've heard stories about – a whirlpool.

TELEMACHUS	A what?
ATHENE	A large amount of water moving in a circle.
TELEMACHUS	I know what a whirlpool is Mentis.
ATHENE	Which may – if the stories are true – hurl us down to the Halls of Eternal Rest.
TELEMACHUS	Oh Gods! Is there no end to this adventure? (*silence*) Giving up is a perfectly intelligent response to this situation.
ATHENE	Perfectly. It's just the wrong thing to do.
TELEMACHUS	Tie me to the mast.
ATHENE	(*kisses him*) Thank you. (*She ties him to the mast.*)
TELEMACHUS	What about you?
ATHENE	Don't worry about me.
TELEMACHUS	Well I do – actually.
ATHENE	I will hold on for dear life.

Music – lights change. They are at sea.

TELEMACHUS	Mentis?
ATHENE	Yes?
TELEMACHUS	What if the stories aren't true? What if we simply reach the edge of the world – and fall off – into space.
ATHENE	In that case – we should say goodbye.
TELEMACHUS	Goodbye Mentis.
ATHENE	Master…

The raft spins and the sound of the whirlpool gets louder and louder. They cry out. Blackout. The Halls of the Dead. Lights rise. TELEMACHUS *is slumped unconscious and still tied to the mast.* Mentis *has vanished around* Telemachus. *Lights flicker, which represent the strange shape of the spirits who walk in the Halls of the Dead. Behind* Telemachus *a shadowy figure in rags approaches.*

TELEMACHUS   (*wakes*) Who's there? Mentis? Is that you? (*He sees* Odysseus.) Who are you? Stay where you are. (Odysseus *approaches and takes* Telemachus' *sword. He looks at it for a moment and then cuts the boy free and puts the sword down.*) Are you, one of the dead?

ODYSSEUS   Sometimes I think so.

TELEMACHUS   What is your name? (*There is a low moan from the spirits.*) What was that?

ODYSSEUS   The moans of the dead. The unhappy ones can kick up a terrible din sometimes.

TELEMACHUS   There are so many.

ODYSSEUS   They are without number.

TELEMACHUS   But you. You're not one of them. Are you?

ODYSSEUS   Not yet – I – I work here.

TELEMACHUS   Ah!

ODYSSEUS   Though it has to be said there's not much work to be done. In fact, I've been waiting for someone to visit. Is there some long-departed soul you wished to talk to?

TELEMACHUS   I'm looking for my father.

ODYSSEUS   His name?

TELEMACHUS   Odysseus.

ODYSSEUS   Odysseus isn't here. He isn't dead, though he might wish it so.

TELEMACHUS   I must find him.

ODYSSEUS	And you are?
TELEMACHUS	His son, Telemachus.
ODYSSEUS	He didn't tell me he had a son. Strange, for he was here and we talked at length.
TELEMACHUS	Why would he come to this cold and lonely place?
ODYSSEUS	Curiosity, and to talk to a few old friends. (TELEMACHUS *breaks down and weeps.*) Why do you weep so?
TELEMACHUS	Because I hate him. I hate him.
ODYSSEUS	Why do you search for him then?

Silence.

TELEMACHUS	Do you know where he was going? Did he say?
ODYSSEUS	No. He had no plans for the future. Please, stay and speak with me. I am no-one but I am someone.
TELEMACHUS	I haven't time. I must follow him.
ODYSSEUS	You have all the time – time does not pass here. It has ceased to be. You can't waste it or spend it wisely. Besides you need to rest. You're very tired.
TELEMACHUS	You said my father spoke to someone, one of the dead.
ODYSSEUS	Achilles. The Hero of the Greeks. Who died at Troy. Do you wish to speak to him?
TELEMACHUS	Achilles?
ODYSSEUS	See there he is...

A light rises on a vision of ACHILLES.

Still covered in blood and bitter wounds as on the day he died.

TELEMACHUS *turns away from him.*

Come I'm sure you'd like to speak to him. He's every boy's Hero, but you must offer him this bowl of blood to drink and then he may speak again as he did in life, otherwise he will remain the voiceless shadow that you see.

TELEMACHUS *takes the bowl and gives it to* ACHILLES, *who drinks.*

ACHILLES	Who are you?
TELEMACHUS	Telemachus, son of Odysseus and Penelope.
ACHILLES	Telemachus? Why have you come?
TELEMACHUS	I'm searching for my father. He was here.
ACHILLES	Yes, the old trickster, master of landways and seaways. (*He smiles.*)
TELEMACHUS	Why? Why did he come here?
ACHILLES	Since he had no friends left in the world above, he came to make peace with those in the world below. In life, we were friends, but we argued and became enemies.
TELEMACHUS	But why? Over what?
ACHILLES	It's strange – I – I can't remember. Thus all anger fades. (*pause*) Why are you searching Telemachus?
TELEMACHUS	I don't know anymore. I've looked for him so long, come so far, and now I no longer know the reason. He abandoned me and my mother, to fight a war he said would make us rich. When it was over instead of coming home, as he had promised, he went off on a – cruise – an adventure. He lived life to the full, for pleasure. Those who helped him, he cheated – those who loved him, he abused, and the men who trusted him and sailed with him, they all died. He sacrificed them all so that he might see the world, and what

has he seen? Witches, giants, ghosts. And he never
came home as he promised, or made any effort to
come home and my mother was driven half-mad with
anxiety, loneliness and fear, why do I want to find him?
I don't.

ACHILLES   Telemachus, let me speak to you as if you were my
own son. Hear my words and let them remain with
you all the days of your life. Here am I, the greatest
soldier of a great army. These are my wounds. Behind
me are many others whom I have killed with these
hands. I – like your father, was in love with death – but
now I would rather be a poor man ploughing a poor
field than King of the lifeless dead. Do not lead the life
we led, Telemachus. But go – find your father, for he
lives, but be swift for death pursues him like a winged
dog and snaps at his heels. Do not give up the search,
for the search is life, and for all its sorrows life is good.

The image of ACHILLES *fades,* ODYSSEUS *steps forward, having
heard all of this.*

TELEMACHUS   I believed in him. I loved the idea of him, and he never
came home.

ODYSSEUS   It was a long war Telemachus – at Troy. It wasn't what
we thought it would be. It destroyed us, it made
demons of us or adventurers or beggars. For ten years
we knew nothing but death. We dreamed so hard for
home, and love and life that in the end they became
dreams, and war alone was real. Every day we watched
our friends die, like brave Achilles and every day a
little bit of ourselves slipped away until we were no
longer men but the shells of men, capable of any
cruelty. Finally we defeated the Trojans with a trick.
My clever trick for which I am renowned. A wooden
horse, pregnant with death, which the Trojans pulled
inside their city walls. My 'trick' that led to victory,

and to the murder of a thousand men, women and children. I became an empty space Telemachus, where victory had no meaning. I could not fill that space, wherever I went, whatever wonders I beheld and I have seen all the wonders of our world – I could not then fill the empty space inside me. Don't you know me Telemachus? My son.

TELEMACHUS   You are not my father.

ODYSSEUS   Perhaps I'm not what you expected, but I am your father. For that I apologise.

TELEMACHUS   You cannot be. You cannot be.

ODYSSEUS   And yet I am.

TELEMACHUS   No.

ODYSSEUS   No? These hands built the house in which you were born. I laid the lintel of oak across the door myself – at that door I trust my foolish dog still sits waiting for me. His name is Argos.

TELEMACHUS   No! (*He attacks* ODYSSEUS, *who barely tries to defend himself.*)

ODYSSEUS   (*flatly*) Kill me then. Kill me. I welcome it. For I hate myself more than you will ever hate me. (TELEMACHUS *turns away.*) My son?

TELEMACHUS   Don't call me that! Ever.

ODYSSEUS   You should not have come here. (*silence*) How did you pass the whirlpool?

TELEMACHUS   I tied myself to the mast.

ODYSSEUS   The Cyclops?

TELEMACHUS   I killed him – with this. (*He holds up the Golden Sword.*) Which was given to me by the Goddess of Ogygia, who is called Calypso. Remember? And this (*the shield*) was given me by a girl – not much older than I. (*He spits in his father's face.*) These are not the questions you should be asking me, father. Ask me of Ithaca. Ask me about your wife – Penelope.

ODYSSEUS   Penelope?

TELEMACHUS   Is dead. (*pause*) And her death belongs to you. She's here among these cold shadows. Why don't you summon her and tell her why you never came home. (*silence*)

ODYSSEUS   How did she die?

TELEMACHUS   A man named Eurymachus has taken your house, land and wealth. He would have taken your wife too, but she stopped him.

ODYSSEUS   She killed herself?

TELEMACHUS   What? Aren't you sad, no tears?

ODYSSEUS   Go home Telemachus.

TELEMACHUS   Home?

ODYSSEUS   I don't deserve the risks you've taken to find me. I'm not worthy of you, or her.

TELEMACHUS   But you must be, you must, you promised.

ODYSSEUS   Leave me. This is where I belong for I am dead in all but name. (*He sinks to his knees.*)

TELEMACHUS   No. (*He pulls his father up.*) You will come home and do what you should have done a long time ago.

ODYSSEUS   I can't. I can't. (*He pulls away from* TELEMACHUS.) You do not know how easy it is to lose the way. Telemachus?

Enter ATHENE *at speed. She tries to pull from* ODYSSEUS *a bag which he has around his neck. He grabs her.*

TELEMACHUS	Mentis.
ODYSSEUS	What's this?
ATHENE	Villain, robber, liar, thief.
ODYSSEUS	So I am. And you?
ATHENE	I am one to be scared of.

ODYSSEUS *laughs.*

TELEMACHUS	This is my servant Mentis. Let her go.
ATHENE	You heard him. (*He drops her. But she has the bag.*) Ah!
ODYSSEUS	Those are my things. Give them back – Give them back!
ATHENE	Correction – these are my things. How dare you steal from the Gods, Odysseus, son of Laertes. (*She holds up a pair of golden shoes with small wings upon them.*)
ODYSSEUS	Athene?
TELEMACHUS	Mentis?
ODYSSEUS	This is no servant – this is Athene, Immortal Goddess, daughter of Zeus, God of Gods.
TELEMACHUS	Don't be daft.
ATHENE	(*She now lifts her arms. Thunder and lightning strike.* ODYSSEUS *kneels before her.*) So Odysseus, old knife, master of landways and seaways, you have caused me a deal of discomfort. You stole my shoes.
ODYSSEUS	I was merely keeping them safe until…
ATHENE	My sword you gave to a witch. My shield you gave to a pubescent princess. (*She recovers these items.*)
ODYSSEUS	But your shoes…

ATHENE	Because of you I have been turned into a pig, tossed into the sea, I have felt cold, hot, frightened, jealous and very very hungry. Me a Goddess. What excuse can you give me?
ODYSSEUS	I did what I did to survive. Now that you've been human, if only for a little while, perhaps you'll understand what it's like to know there is an end to life, that time runs against you. (*silence*)
ATHENE	You – why did I ever choose to champion such a smooth-talking Greek?
TELEMACHUS	This is ridiculous.

She points to him and TELEMACHUS *feels as if he's been stabbed and cries out.*

ATHENE	I am very annoyed.
ODYSSEUS	Great Athene, thank you for the loan of your golden armour, they were my protection on a perilous voyage. I praise your generosity and am your obedient servant.
ATHENE	Then go home, with your Son, to Ithaca.
CHORUS	(*sing*) ITHACA
ATHENE	My father Zeus, Master of Gods and Men, grant me once again my Godlike powers, for I have found the golden gifts that were only yours to give. Know then that I am your daughter Athene, Goddess of the grey eyes.

Low rumble of thunder. Lightning strikes. ATHENE *receives her full powers.*

ATHENE	Now over rock and sea we fly where the young dawn comes bright in the east. Even now she spreads her fingertips of rose upon the Isle of Ithaca.
CHORUS	(*sing*) ITHACA – HOME.

71

Ithaca.

ODYSSEUS *and* TELEMACHUS *are back in Ithaca.* ATHENE *has vanished. Enter* EURYCLEIA.

EURYCLEIA	Master. Oh it's true then, you have come home.
TELEMACHUS	Good Eurycleia.
EURYCLEIA	Safe an' well. (*She embraces him several times.*) An' still alive.
TELEMACHUS	Only just. Now be swift and tell me how things stand here in Ithaca.
EURYCLEIA	Your father?
TELEMACHUS	I couldn't find him.
EURYCLEIA	Heaven preserve us then – what are we to do?
TELEMACHUS	(*takes her to one side*) How is my mother?
EURYCLEIA	As the day you left her, caught in a sleep that looks like death. This potion will wake her.
TELEMACHUS	Then go and do so.
EURYCLEIA	But Master?
TELEMACHUS	Do as I command.
EURYCLEIA	Command? I will not – for all your impudence. Eurymachus thinks her dead and buried. If she wakes heaven alone knows what he might do. He's taken control of Ithaca. No-one calls him King but he is King right enough and rules most coldly. He allows no repairs to the house, the fields are left to weeds, the vineyards be all collapsed. It's as if he willed his own

72

destruction. Oh if only you had found your father. Who is this?

TELEMACHUS   No-one. A beggar, I picked up on my travels.

EURYCLEIA   Can he be trusted?

TELEMACHUS   Who can tell? Go and wake my mother.

EURYCLEIA   But I have told you how things stand with Eurymachus. You must leave again for he will come straight here to murder you the moment he hears of your arrival.

TELEMACHUS   I'll take my chance with Eurymachus. I have survived ordeals that make a man of his stature shrink to a very common size of foe. Please Eurycleia, wake my mother.

EURYCLEIA   Yes master.

TELEMACHUS   Be quick – Eurymachus approaches.

Exit EURYCLEIA.

Enter EURYMACHUS.

EURYMACHUS   Telemachus, welcome. You have some nerve, to come back here. I'm impressed, but there must be a reason for such foolishness.

TELEMACHUS   To banish you from my house.

EURYMACHUS   You don't have a house Telemachus. This is my house. But for old times sake I will allow you to be buried here. Next to your mother?

TELEMACHUS *turns and picks up the two spears which have been used throughout in the dream fights.*

EURYMACHUS   Ah – you came to fight. Brave boy.

TELEMACHUS   No – your fight is not with me Eurymachus but with my father.

EURYMACHUS	(*turns and sees* ODYSSEUS *who now steps out of the shadows*) This – rag…?
TELEMACHUS	Is my father.
EURYMACHUS	(*laughs*) I know your father well and I swear by all the gods this is not he. You've been tricked.
TELEMACHUS	Believe me Eurymachus this is my father. (*He gives* ODYSSEUS *a spear.*) He will fight you and kill you or if he has no reason to live and loves not himself or his son or the memory of his wife, then you may kill him.
ODYSSEUS	Telemachus – please.
TELEMACHUS	Don't you love me father? (*silence*) Then fight for yourself. Fight for your own life.
ODYSSEUS	Would you have me shed more blood for something which has no meaning?
TELEMACHUS	Then fight for your house, your crops, your vineyards, your many servants who need you.

Silence.

EURYMACHUS	As I said, this is not your father.
TELEMACHUS	I need you, mother needs you.
ODYSSEUS	But she's dead, and I'm responsible.
TELEMACHUS	No, no, she isn't dead, she lives, she lives.

Music. Enter PENELOPE *on* EURYCLEIA's *arm. She can barely stand.*

EURYMACHUS	What magic is this? What drug have you fed me that I see ghosts?
ODYSSEUS	Penelope?
EURYMACHUS	This is some deadly vision. She is dead.
TELEMACHUS	No. You see father. She is alive. She is alive.

EURYMACHUS	It cannot be so. Did I grieve for nothing? If she be not dead, as once she was, she shall be once again. (*He raises his spear against* PENELOPE. EURYCLEIA *stands in his way.*) I will not be tricked. I am King of Ithaca. (*He attacks* ODYSSEUS. ODYSSEUS *overwhelms him and puts his spear to his throat.*)
ODYSSEUS	I am Odysseus, King of Ithaca, Lord of my lands and house, to which my son has so bravely brought me, with more love and tenderness than a father such as I deserve. In his name and in the name of my wife, Penelope, whom I have treated with great disdain, I give you your life.
TELEMACHUS	Father?
ODYSSEUS	Shall I deny this man the gift you have given me? Go Eurymachus, and though you be banished from this island, believe me it is small, and the world is large and there is much to see and you may find hope in the strangest of places.

EURYMACHUS *stretches out his hands to* PENELOPE. *She turns away. He exits.*

ODYSSEUS	My wife.
PENELOPE	(*looks at him, then walks past him to* TELEMACHUS) Telemachus – you seem – so changed.
EURYCLEIA	Be careful my lady. (*She hugs her son.*)
ODYSSEUS	Penelope.
PENELOPE	(*Turns and slaps the face of* ODYSSEUS. *He kneels.*) Do not kneel to me. (*He stands.*) Nor stand, nor sit nor anything. (*silence*) But come to my chambers tomorrow when I have had some hours to gather in the storm which rages in me against you. (*She falls and* EURYCLEIA *is about to help her up but* ODYSSEUS *offers his arm. After a moment she takes it.*)

ODYSSEUS   Let me help you.

Exit ODYSSEUS *and* PENELOPE.

EURYCLEIA   What did he expect, a meal on the table? (TELEMACHUS *breathes a sigh of relief.*) I suppose you are hungry then, after all your adventures?

TELEMACHUS   Yes I am – I am.

EURYCLEIA   Brave boy.

TELEMACHUS   You knew it was my father all along. Didn't you?

EURYCLEIA   They say a person's eyes are a mirror of their soul, but that's rubbish, he had a scar on his forehead which I recognised immediately. All I saw in his eyes, was pain, an' a good portion of it.

TELEMACHUS   What do you think will happen between them?

EURYCLEIA   Who knows, but I do know it's not in your hands. You are not responsible for their happiness. Understood. Some food then – it'll have to be simple – I'm all of a flutter.

TELEMACHUS   Some bread, some cheese.

ATHENE   (*from under the bed*) And pickle.

EURYCLEIA   (*turns back*) You don't like pickle.

TELEMACHUS   Well I am more adventurous than I used to be – and some wine.

EURYCLEIA   Oh I say, some 'wine'. We have grown up. I'm glad to have you home, master. There's work to be done here, to make this house well again – but I am optimistic, that's my nature – tis very foolish, but there tis. (*She goes to leave and turns back.*) By the way, whatever happened to that boy you left with? That friend of yours, who came out of nowhere?

Telemachus Ah – well the boy turned into a girl, and the girl turned into a goddess.

Eurycleia I see. (*aside*) Anyone would think I was born yesterday.

Exit Eurycleia.

Enter Athene.

Athene Telemachus – the old sea dog.

Telemachus Mentis. (*They embrace, as the best of friends, but then* Telemachus *backs away.*) Athene.

Athene I came to thank you.

Telemachus Me?

Athene And to give you this. (*She gives him a golden sword.*)

Telemachus But your father…

Athene Has agreed – you deserve to keep the sword.

Telemachus Thank you.

Athene Use it wisely or it will turn against you. So, what are you going to do now?

Telemachus I don't know. I thought I might pick up a boat headed east. I'll go east and east again. See a few sights.

Athene You only just got home.

Telemachus I can always come back.

Athene Not always, things happen. Your father had no way back until you found him.

Telemachus He and I are – strangers, and whatever he says I can't forgive him. I can't.

Athene You owe him nothing it's true, but give him a little time to prove himself. Do this for me, after all I am his foolish Champion. Goodbye Telemachus. I shall never

forget our journey and what it felt like to be – so utterly
lost. The Gods bless you, and your house, and the Isle
of Ithaca.

CHORUS   (*sing*) ITHACA

Exit ATHENE.

TELEMACHUS   Athene!

Silence.

Enter ODYSSEUS.

ODYSSEUS   Telemachus?

TELEMACHUS   Yes father?

*They remain standing, with some distance between them as
the lights fade to blackout.*

Activities

Before you study the play
Independent research: *The Odyssey*

This play unfolds against the background of the journey of Odysseus, retelling an ancient tale in a modern way. Before you study the play, you should know about Odysseus and his journey.

1 In pairs, devise a series of ten questions that you have about the original tale, *The Odyssey*. List them in a table like the one below.

2 Use the internet or your library to help you find out the information you need to answer your questions. Remember to list your sources of information, as in the example below.

Question	Answer	Source
1 Who wrote The Odyssey?	A Roman poet called Homer	Wikipedia
2 When was The Odyssey written?		

Independent research: Greek gods and goddesses

When reading the play, it will be helpful if you know about the Greek gods and goddesses who play a part in the drama. As a class, you are going to create a display board of informative posters about each of the characters.

1 Make a list of all the gods and goddesses that are mentioned in the play.

2 Share out the main characters between small groups, so that each character is covered. In your group, conduct some brief research into the character you have been allocated.

3 Use your research to create an informative poster about the character. You may wish to make use of photographs, illustrations or diagrams to present your research and you should think about how to present your writing so that it is easy for other students to read.

4 As a class, spend some time looking at each poster so that everyone is familiar with the characters. You may also wish to share your information orally, giving a short presentation on what you have learned about your characters.

Active reading strategies: practising pronunciation

As you read the play's character list, you will notice that there are many unusual names.

1 Identify the patterns of vowels, such as *eu*, and the patterns of consonants, such as *ry*, that are less common in English words.
2 In pairs, work out how you think you would say each name, writing it out phonetically as it would be said. For example, Telemachus could be written phonetically as Tel-em-mack-us. (Hint: *ch* is pronounced as *k* and an *e* at the end of a word is sounded out.)
3 As a class, agree how these words should be said and then practise saying them.

Act 1
Active reading strategies: clarifying ideas

When the Trojan war is over, Odysseus chooses to go on a voyage. Work with a partner to create a PMI table as if you are Odysseus at the end of the Trojan war. You will need to outline the positives of going on a voyage, the minuses of such a voyage and any interesting questions you might have. Use the examples below to start you off.

Positives	Minuses	Interesting questions
It gives you time to consider the consequences of all the warring.	It means you cannot return home to your wife and son.	Should you go home to get them first, before embarking on your voyage of self-discovery?

Active reading strategies: exploring characters' viewpoints

On page 4, Telemachus spars with his mother's suitor, Eurymachus. Telemachus says, 'One day, my Father will come home and cut your head off.' As a reader, you can establish a relationship with a character by thinking about their motivations and emotions. For instance, if we can understand how Telemachus feels about his father's continued absence, it will help us to understand his character better.

1   In pairs, make a list of questions that you would like to ask Telemachus about his father, for example: How do you feel about your father going away for such a long time?

2   Predict how Telemachus would answer your questions. Write your questions and his answers as an interview script.

3   As a class, pool your questions. Identify common questions you want to ask Telemachus and explore the answers that other students gave. This will help you develop your ability to interpret how characters' actions and words can be seen in a range of ways.

Writing a narrative commentary

At many points in the play, Telemachus hears about his father's adventures from people who have been with Odysseus.

1   Reread pages 6 to 8, where the messenger tells of Odysseus's victories in Troy.

2   Write a narrative account of a fictional battle leading up to this victory. You should write as if you are the messenger and describe Odysseus's actions in battle. You may wish to do this in the style of a sports commentary, as if you are commentating on the action as it happens.

Active reading strategies: inferring meaning

On page 9, Athene describes Telemachus and Penelope watching for Odysseus's return, saying 'Each day mother and son gazed out to sea until all those who had escaped sheer destruction, either by land or by sea came home, all but one man alone.'

1 Develop your inference skills by imagining what Telemachus would be thinking as he sits looking out to sea, expecting Odysseus to return, yet never seeing him. Create a large thought bubble on paper. Add Telemachus's thoughts, such as *I wonder what has happened to my father*, on the inside of the thought bubble.

2 Use the outside of the thought bubble to note the feelings that Telemachus might have, such as fear.

Drama techniques: mime

When constructing dramatic scenes, particularly those that feature battles or fights, it is important to think about the choreography. Stage actors spend time rehearsing and choreographing their movements so that they are not only good representations of the action, but also to try to use movement in creative and imaginative ways. In Act 1, on page 12, mime is used to retell the story of Odysseus's fight with Achilles.

1 With a partner, create a mime of Odysseus's fight with Achilles using the stage directions to guide you. Make sure your actions are smooth, seamless and well-rehearsed. You may also wish to choose a suitable piece of music to accompany your mime.

2 Once you have perfected the choreography of your mime, you may wish to perform it to an audience, comparing your performance with another pair's interpretation.

Active reading strategies: considering characters' viewpoints

1   Reread the conversation between Telemachus and Penelope on pages 18 to 19.

2   Draw a continuum line like the one below with a scale from 0 to 10. Consider where each character would stand in terms of their hope for Odysseus's safe return, with 0 representing no hope and 10 representing complete hope that he will return.

3   Find evidence from the passage so that you are sure your views are based on the text.

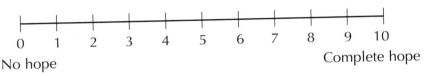

0   1   2   3   4   5   6   7   8   9   10

No hope   Complete hope

Drama techniques: dramatic presentation

1   With a partner, consider how hopeful Telemachus and Penelope feel that Odysseus will return in the scene on pages 18 to 19 where Penelope tells her son that she is considering remarrying.

2   You are going to act out this scene, from 'My son, I need to talk to you...' to 'I promise.' Discuss how you can use your voices to show Telemachus's and Penelope's emotions. Think about how you can convey the characters' feelings through their tone of voice.

3   Practise reading the lines aloud, adding the appropriate expression, volume and tone to make sure the audience knows how your character is feeling as he or she considers Odysseus's return.

Act 2

Writing to imagine, entertain and explore

You are going to write imaginatively about a stormy scene at sea. To help you prepare for this, you may wish to use visual material such as documentaries about storms at sea or films like 'The Perfect Storm'.

1 To plan your writing, consider all the things you could see, hear and smell if you were on a boat in the middle of a stormy sea. Add them, as nouns, to the directional prepositions on a map like the one below. You should include things you can see like the waves, as well as things such as thunder that you can hear and things you can smell like the wet wood of the boat.

2 Now add adjectives to your diagram that describe the nouns you have chosen. For instance, you may choose to add *rumbling* to thunder. You may also choose to add other figurative language to your map, including similes, metaphors and personification.

3 Having completed your plan, begin to write your account in full sentences, using the directional prepositions to help you link between one idea and the next. You may wish to use some of these to start off your sentences, but don't forget your commas! For example: *Above us, the rumbling thunder shattered the sky, booming and rolling.*

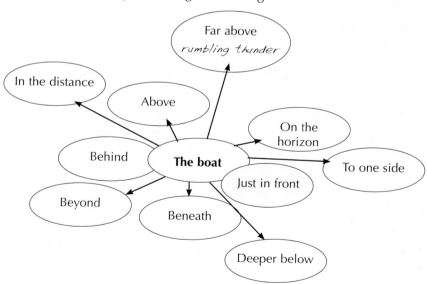

Activities

Writing to persuade, argue and advise

On page 23, Athene tells Telemachus how his father convinced his men to go on the voyage 'West and west again to the edge of the world.' Telemachus doesn't understand why his father would have gone or what he would have said to his men to convince them.

1 Look back at the PMI table on page 81 and think about how you could use this technique to map out the arguments for going, as well as how Odysseus might speak to overcome his men's fears about the journey.

2 Imagine you are Odysseus. Write a short speech, summing up some of these arguments. What explanation could he give for his reasons? How might you use some persuasive devices, such as rhetorical questions, to help you construct your argument?

Active reading strategies: clarifying ideas

Telemachus is faced with a difficult decision on pages 32 to 34, when Calypso pleads with him to stay. You are going to explore the ways Calypso tries to persuade Telemachus, by looking at what she says to him and what she does to convince him to stay.

1 Work with a partner to identify the arguments Calypso uses to persuade Telemachus to stay with her. List them in the first column of a table like the one below.

2 In the second column, speculate on what Telemachus's reactions to Calypso's persuasion are likely to be. Think about what would be going through Telemachus's mind when she says what she does. An example has been completed for you.

3 Share your ideas with another pair and explore the different ways you think Telemachus would respond to Calypso's arguments. Which arguments do you think he would find most convincing?

4 Before you read on, consider whether you think Telemachus will stay or not, and give your reasons. You may wish to record your predictions as a class before you continue studying the play.

Calypso's argument	Telemachus' reaction
It would be such fun to have a child around the place.	I'd love to be a child and not have any responsibilities. A child has so much more freedom than an adult. But I'm no longer a child.

Act 3

Writing to inform, explain and describe

You have been asked to write a fact sheet about one of the Greek gods, aimed at primary school readers. For example, you may choose to explore the character of Poseidon, as he is a key figure in Act 3.

1 Decide how you will present your fact sheet to help your primary school readers make the most of the information you are sharing with them. Consider how you will break the text up, how to use illustrations and what features you could use to help readers find their way around the sheet.

2 Consider the language you will need to use to make sure your readers can understand the information easily. Make four or five decisions about this, thinking about the tone of your writing. For example:

- How will you involve your reader and make the fact sheet interesting and enjoyable?
- How will you make the more difficult information easy to understand?
- How will you make the writing appropriate for the reading abilities of the audience?

3 Finally, consider the way you are going to organise your writing to make it easy to follow. How can you use headings and sub-headings to present your ideas?

4 Once you have made these decisions, carry out some research and make notes on your chosen Greek god.

5 Organise and write the information in the form of a fact sheet, making sure it is appropriate for primary school readers.

6 When you have completed your fact sheet, share it with a partner, explaining what decisions you took and how these can be seen in your final piece of writing.

Writing a recount

There are many ways that you can recount the various actions undertaken by Odysseus. Most of what Telemachus knows about his father has been recounted to him by other people.

1 Choose a style of recount that would be appropriate for television or radio, for example a sports commentary, news report or documentary voice-over.

2 Write a recount of Odysseus's fight with the Cyclops (described on page 52). The following is an example written in the style of a wrestling match commentary.

Odysseus enters the arena now, looking mean and moody. People say he hasn't got a chance against the Cyclops, who must outweigh him by a good three hundred pounds. But Odysseus has a brilliant track record - nobody expected him to get as far as he has. It'll be a close fight, that's for sure. Polyphemus has been angered by all this prematch banter and it'll be good to see the old one-eyed giant back at his top performance.

And here comes Odysseus now, with a posse of his best Argonauts around him. Polyphemus has his burning spikes out. Oh, and there goes the first Argonaut - straight through the heart. That's got to hurt!

Act 4

Active reading strategies: making judgements

In order to explore your perspective on Odysseus and your understanding of the play, it is important that you make judgements.

1   Your teacher will display the words 'resourceful' and 'trickster' at opposite ends of the classroom. Individually, decide which of these words best describes Odysseus and go to the appropriate side of the classroom.

2   When everyone has chosen a side, discuss your reasons for making your choices.

3   Think about the two words 'resourceful' and 'trickster'. What do they have in common? What separates them and makes them different? Share your ideas as a class.

Active reading strategies: exploring characters' viewpoints

On pages 66 and 67, Telemachus talks to Achilles about his father, saying 'He abandoned me and my mother, to fight a war he said would make us rich... he went off on a cruise – an adventure...'

1   Reread this section of the play, from 'Who are you?' to '...life is good'.

2   In order to explore the text in more detail, you should understand the characters' perspectives on events and actions. Draw a large thought bubble on a piece of paper and divide it in two. On one side, list all the positive qualities, such as bravery, you think Telemachus would see in his father and, on the other side, list all the negative qualities.

3   Share your diagram with a partner and discuss any differences and similarities.

4   Reread Odysseus's description of his journey on pages 67 and 68. Add the reasons he gives for his journey to either the positive or the negative side of your thought bubble.

Active reading strategies: asking questions

On page 67, Telemachus meets Odysseus, although he doesn't know who he is.

1 What questions do you think Telemachus would want to ask his father? Make a list of possible questions.

2 How do you think Odysseus would reply? Jot down some notes about Odysseus's likely answers.

3 In pairs, take it in turn to play the role of Odysseus and hot-seat each other using the questions and answers you have prepared.

After you have studied the play

Active reading strategies: developing thinking

Using an A–Z table is a good way to review all the main characters, themes and ideas in the play in order to gain an overview of the whole text.

1 Work as a group of three or four. On a piece of A3 paper, construct a table with two columns and thirteen rows. Put one letter of the alphabet in each box, so that each box contains a different letter.

2 As a group, add three or four ideas, places, characters or themes to each box. Use the example below to help start your thinking.

3 When you have finished your poster, you may like to share your thinking with the class or another group.

A Athene, adventure, armour, anxiety	B
C Calypso	D disappointment
E	F fury

Drama techniques: sets, props and costumes

Working in a small group, you are going to solve the problem of how to bring the play to life visually on stage by devising a set and choosing props and costumes. You may wish to present these as a design board.

1 This play is set in a variety of locations with different landscapes, which would need to be represented on stage. Devise a set that could be used for all the major scenes in the play.

2 Draw up a list of props that will be needed to help the audience imagine the setting more clearly.

3 Devise appropriate costumes for each of the characters.

Active reading strategies: exploring characters

One way of understanding a character is to consider what facts we know about them and what additional information we can infer about them from what they say and do.

1 Work with a partner or as a small group to explore the character of Telemachus further. Draw an outline of him on a large sheet of paper.

2 Inside the outline, write ten key quotations from across the whole play that tell us about Telemachus's character. For instance, 'He will come home and sweep you from the house like so many dead leaves' (page 5).

3 Next to each quotation, write a word that explains what this tells us about Telemachus, for example *arrogant* or *proud*.

Information retrieval

1 List the main events of the play in the order that they happen, making sure that you include them all. Here are two examples.

Athene argues with her father, Zeus, because she feels sorry for Odysseus.

Zeus says he has not forgotten Odysseus but it is Poseidon who is angry with Odysseus for blinding his son, Polyphemus, the Cyclops.

2 Create a timeline of the events to show Odysseus's journey in a visual way. An example section is shown below. You will notice that the facts in the play are not in chronological order. For instance, at the beginning we meet Telemachus and yet we hear about events that have happened in other countries while he was growing up. We only hear about Odysseus's journey as it is revealed to Telemachus throughout the play.

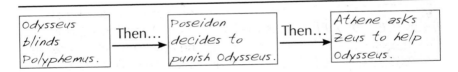

Active reading strategies: comparing and contrasting characters

1 Make a list of the characteristics that Odysseus and Telemachus have demonstrated during the play.

2 Consider which qualities they share and which are personal to each character. For instance, you could say that both Odysseus and Telemachus are adventurous. Construct a Venn diagram, like the one below, to plot their characteristics, showing which ones they share and which are personal to each character.

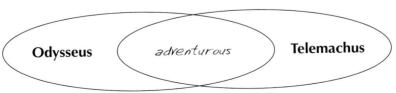

If you enjoyed reading *The Search for Odysseus*, why not try...

Shadow of the Minotaur by Alan Gibbons

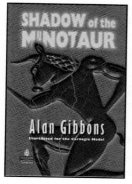

Phoenix is a death-defying hero of the Greek myths, battling Medusa and the invincible Minotaur ... but only when he's not being bullied at school. Phoenix leads two lives – 'real life' and his adventures inside the virtual reality game *The Legendeer*. But *The Legendeer* is more than a game and soon captures Phoenix in its deadly maze ...

ISBN 978 0 582 84869 6

The Conch Bearer by Chitra Banerjee Divakaruni

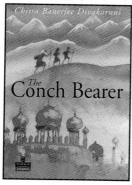

A classic quest story set in India. Ill luck forces twelve-year-old Anand to support his family until one day he meets a strange beggar who demands Anand's help to protect a treasure of immeasurable value – a tiny beautiful conch shell. But this is no ordinary conch; it has a potent magical force and must be returned to its rightful home.

ISBN 978 1 4058 1648 9

Wolf Brother by Michelle Paver

A tense and thrilling adventure novel that takes you back in time to a pre-historic world of hunter-gatherers, tribes and unearthly superstitions. With his father's dying words ringing in his ears, Torak knows that time is running out. Soon, the demon bear will kill again. Nothing is safe. But Torak won't be alone in the Forest for long. Strangers lurk between the whispering trees, eyes watching his every move. With only an orphaned wolf cub for company, Torak must keep his promise to find the Mountain.

ISBN 978 1 4058 2271 8

The search for Odysseus

- Odysseus goes off to war leaving his wife Penelope, and his son Telemachus

- He tells Penelope that if he hasn't ~~come~~ returned by the time Telemachus has grown his first beard then she should marry.

- Penelope has this evil person that fancies her, (eurymachus)

- Odysseus doesn't return by the time Telemachus has his first beard, so telemachus goes on a little voyage to find him

- The goddess Athene comes to Telemachus disguised as a little boy.

- Telemachus goes off on his voyage and wakes up on his raft with Athene which he calls ~~me~~ Mentor

- Telemachus wakes up on an island where he finds a goddess called calypso
- calyspo tries to ~~think~~ TRICK him into staying on the island, just like she tried to trick his dad
- when calypso sees that Telemachus is determined to leave the island she stops trying and gives him his father's sword.
- They get shipwrecked and wake up on an island where they find people that odysseus was really mean to when he went there.
- The people on the island tell him that his dad

- went to the land of Cyclops.
- so telemachus follows his follows his dad to the land of the cyclops
- telemachus finds his dad and has a go at him, he finds out who is Mentor is and that it is Athene the goddess
- Athene gets backs the things odysseus took from her
- She tells odysseus to go back home to his wife and family
- He goes back home and everything is fine
- telemachus sees odysseus